SPECIAL EDUCATIONAL NEEDS: THE KEY CONCEPTS

Special Educational Needs: The Key Concepts explores the complex issues that surround SEN both in and out of the classroom. This reader-friendly text considers the impact that these issues have upon the child, the parent, the teacher and the school as a whole.

Fully cross-referenced and including suggestions for further reading with each entry, areas discussed include:

- pupil rights and empowerment
- parents and care workers
- curriculum and teaching
- inclusive approaches
- historical dimensions

Providing an informative combination of practical, historical and legal terms and concepts, this is a highly useful resource accessible to a broad audience.

Philip Garner is Professor of Education at the University of Northampton. He has published widely on issues relating to special education, including *The Handbook of Emotional and Behavioural Difficulties*.

D0549877

TES
11- 2009

Also available from Routledge

Fifty Major Thinkers on Education
Joy Palmer
0-415-23126-4

Fifty Modern Thinkers on Education
Joy Palmer
0-415-22409-8

Key Concepts in the Philosophy of Education
John Gingell and Christopher Winch
0-415-17304-3

Primary Education: The Key Concepts
Denis Hayes
0-415-35483-8

Secondary Education: The Key Concepts
Jerry Wellington
0-415-34403-4

Sport and Physical Education: The Key Concepts
Tim Chandler, Mike Cronin and Wray Vamplew
0-415-23142-6

SPECIAL EDUCATIONAL NEEDS

The Key Concepts

Philip Garner

Routledge
Taylor & Francis Group

LONDON AND NEW YORK

UNIVERSITY OF CHICHESTER

First published 2009
by Routledge
2 Park Square, Milton Park, Abingdon, Oxon OX14 4RN

Simultaneously published in the USA and Canada
by Routledge
270 Madison Ave, New York, NY 10016

Routledge is an imprint of the Taylor & Francis Group, an informa business

© 2009 Philip Garner

Typeset in Series Design Selected by Taylor & Francis Books
Printed and bound in Great Britain by
TJ International Ltd, Padstow, Cornwall

British Library Cataloguing in Publication Data
A catalogue record for this book is available from the British Library

Library of Congress Cataloging in Publication Data
Garner, Philip, 1947–
Special educational needs : the key concepts / Philip Garner.
p. cm. – (Routledge key guides)
Includes bibliographical references.
1. Learning disabled children–Education–Great Britain.
2. Special education–Great Britain. I. Title.
LC4706.G7G37 2009
371.9–dc22

2008037543

ISBN 10: 0-415-20719-3 (hbk)
ISBN 10: 0-415-20720-7 (pbk)
ISBN 10: 0-203-08849-2 (ebk)

ISBN 13: 978-0-415-20719-5 (hbk)
ISBN 13: 978-0-415-20720-1 (pbk)
ISBN 13: 978-0-203-08849-4 (ebk)

This book is for my mother, Mary Marjorie Garner (1919–2008). It is my way of thanking her for being the person chiefly responsible for giving me the opportunity to embark on a career in education and, ultimately, to have the privilege of working in the fields of inclusive and special education.

CONTENTS

LIST OF KEY CONCEPTS

Historical dimensions and current themes

ability and attainment
advocacy and empowerment
child protection
children's rights
cognitive development
controversial issues
delinquency
deviance
disadvantage
disruptive behaviour
early SEN legislation
exclusion
gender differences
genetics
historical 'language' of SEN
importance of history
inclusion and individual rights
integration
models of SEN
nature and nurture
normality and difference
school effectiveness
SEN and globalisation
SEN in history
social class

Definitions and terminology

categories of SEN
(a) communication and interaction

    (i) autism
    (ii) speech and language disorder
    (iii) selective mutism
(b) cognition and learning
    (i) dyslexia
    (ii) (hand)writing difficulties
    (iii) dyscalculia
(c) behaviour, emotional and social
    (i) eating disorders
    (ii) attention deficit (hyperactivity) disorder
    (iii) emotional and behavioural difficulties
(d) sensory and/or physical
    (i) brain damage/injury
    (ii) visual impairment
    (iii) epilepsy

Legislation and policy

Education Act 1944
Education (Handicapped Children) Act 1970
Warnock Report (1978)
Education Act 1981
Education 'Reform' Act 1988
United Nations Convention on the Rights of the Child (1989)
Children Act 1989
Elton Report (1989)
Salamanca Statement (1994)
Code of Practice (1994 and 2001)
Education Act 1996
Green Paper (1997) and Programme of Action (1998)
Inclusive Schooling (2001) (DfES)
Special Educational Needs and Disability Act 2003
Every Child Matters (2004)
Children's Plan (2007)
Bercow Report (2008)

Practice and provision

art therapy
assistive technology
behaviour for learning
behaviour modification

case conference
children's services
conductive education
diagnostic testing
differentiation
drama therapy
early intervention
early years education
Excellence in Cities
extended schools
family therapy
home tuition
hospital schools
identification and assessment
individual education plan
intensive interaction
learning styles
life skills
mainstream schools
multi-sensory approaches
music therapy
National Curriculum
National Strategies (Literacy and Numeracy)
nurture group
paired reading
peer tutoring
Performance Indicators ('P-scales')
play therapy
provision mapping
pupil referral unit
Reading Recovery
residential special education
respite care
sanctions and rewards
School Action and School Action Plus
social and emotional aspects of learning
special schools and settings
statement of SEN
support services
support teaching
team around the child
whole-school SEN policy

Pupils, professionals and parents

child and adolescent mental health services
class teacher
educational psychologist
health visitor
home–school relationship
initial teacher training
learning mentor
occupational therapist
parent partnership
physiotherapist
professional collaboration
professional development national standards
professional support
SEN governor
SEN Tribunal
special educational needs coordinator
speech and language therapist
teaching assistant

INTRODUCTION

This book is all about children and young people who are 'different'. It explores the ideas, concepts, policies and processes through which we have sought to address the increasingly diverse ways in which learning and social performances are manifest in schools and other settings. There is no intention to provide a comprehensive coverage of every aspect of what has always been viewed as a complex and multidimensional part of the field of 'education' as a whole. Nevertheless, a set of over 100 terms, approaches, definitions, historical events, policies and controversial issues have been compiled in order to give the reader a real sense of the core *concepts* in special educational needs (SEN), all of which have links to practical manifestations in educational provision for children and young people who experience learning difficulties of one kind or another.

SEN is now a commonly used expression to refer to the difficulties in learning that are encountered by a significant minority of a school's population. The barriers experienced by them can be linked to individual physiological, psychological, social or environmental factors, or a combination of several of these. SEN is an aspect of education which has always tended to bring with it controversy and questions regarding rights, equality and social justice. The book seeks to explore some of the themes and concepts which underpin these from both a theoretical and practical orientation. In doing this it considers five groupings of topics:

1 Historical dimensions and current themes
2 Definitions and terminology
3 Legislation and policy
4 Practice and provision
5 Pupils, professionals and parents

Each of these sections is divided further into a significant number of subsections, or 'concepts'. These variously comprise collections of descriptions, emerging issues and reflective commentaries and questions. The latter are intended both to provoke discussion on some of the more controversial terms included in this collection as well as to illustrate the complexities of this aspect of education. In setting out the content in this way it is hoped that you, as a reader who has been interested enough to be drawn to the term 'SEN' as a focus for study and development, will be prompted to examine your own position regarding some of the key concepts that are never far from the surface whenever the phrase is introduced into a conversation on education. To hold an informed personal 'position' on the topics covered in this book is a vital aspect of personal development and enrichment. Hopefully, too, consideration of the various key concepts addressed in this book will simply be a starting point in a more long-term process of engagement with children and young people whose SEN often means that they are marginalised from many of the benefits of modern society.

It is important to provide some guidance on what this book seeks to do (as well as what it is specifically not intended to do), and also to explain in further detail its structure and organisation. *Key Concepts in Special Educational Needs* has been devised and written to give up-to-date information about what experienced SEN practitioners and other stakeholders see as vital issues in this area of work. To arrive at the 100 or so 'key concepts', I talked with experienced professionals in the field of SEN with whom I am in regular contact with as part of my work in SEN in my own university's School of Education. These included teachers, education psychologists, teaching assistants, education administrators in local authorities, officials working for government agencies, and (importantly) with children and young people and their parents and carers. I invited a small group of these contacts – six in all, but representative of the spectrum of professional engagement in SEN – to examine an initial list of SEN 'concepts, ideas, policies and practices' I had generated as a result of my own engagement with the field. My intention was to construct a set of topics which would both be an adequate description of the current nature of the field, but also which was manageable enough in size. I thought that about 100 topics, if selected according to their priority and importance, was an optimum number in this respect. My professional associates, who I thank here, helped me to refine, amend or make deletions to them overall. It is largely due to their informed opinion that the set of concepts which comprise this book has emerged, although mine is the ultimate responsibility if the reader feels that a topic of personal interest to them has been excluded.

The key concepts have been grouped for continuity and coherence. Thus, in most sections I have entered the concepts alphabetically. But there are two exceptions: that part which is devoted to legislation and policy (where the entries are chronological) and the section dealing with Categories of SEN (where the concepts are grouped according to the four categories of need currently being used by key government agencies in England).

There is no hierarchy of importance suggested, other than the fact that the inclusion of a 'concept' in this book indicates its centrality to developing an understanding of the current nature of SEN in England. Each entry has a description and an embedded commentary, which seeks to give information to the reader whilst also pointing to some of the debates or vital questions which the topic raises. Wherever possible cross-referencing between two or more key concepts has been attempted; this technique illustrates not only the complexity of current SEN approaches but also the ecosystemic or interlinked nature of the field. In making this process one which is accessible to the reader, each concept has been visually reinforced in the body of the text: bold text has been used to highlight a concept which can be found elsewhere in the book. A specific reading is also provided for each topic, beyond those which are embedded within the body of the text. This allows the interested reader to drill down further into the complexities of the key concept under consideration, as well as pointing the way to further resources. A 'key question' is posed at the conclusion of each entry, in order to prompt discussion and enable the reader to extend their own responses to the key concept under consideration.

I have chosen to severely restrict the number of textual references used in the description of each concept. The literature of SEN is voluminous, and the ideas and practices that it encompasses are rich with debate, even controversy. It would be all too easy to predicate every phrase or claim within these descriptions with a supporting reference, which would reduce the book to a referential, academic text. Rather, what I have sought to do is provide a flavour of the 'territory' of SEN, capturing its intricacies, challenges and dilemmas; readers who wish to explore further will find some guidance in an extensive bibliography, contained in an appendix. In addition, a set of key internet websites is included, for readers to access as is appropriate to their needs. Where a reference has been used within the text the full citation is included in the main reference at the end of the book.

Readers will notice that the concepts included in this collection vary considerably in the amount of words used to describe them. This should not be taken as an indication that one concept is necessarily more important than another.

At this point it is important to say something about the notion of a 'concept', as used throughout this book. More usually a 'concept' is taken to mean an idea, a thought or a notion. It can also refer to a 'scheme' or a 'plan'. The term itself originates from the Latin word *conceptus*, which is the past-participle of *concipere*, meaning to conceive. The 'concepts' featured in this book are, in fact, a combination of both 'ideas' and concrete 'plans'. Thus, some of the topics will be discussed in relation to, for example, a piece of SEN legislation, or a practical approach to meeting learner needs. Others will be dealt with more theoretically, as abstract terms which have meaning and impact in the field of SEN. Both 'idea' and 'plan' are subsumed as part of the topic commentary, enabling the reader to see the crucial linkages between thinking and practice.

The first set of key concepts covers aspects of history and a set of current themes which, it is worth noting, remain as a contextual backdrop to current thinking and provision in SEN. That these do have their origins in history is a point well worth making, and emphasises the value of exploring the past as a means of reflecting on contemporary arrangements in SEN. The section then provides a number of overarching themes which seem to have origins as part of the 'history' of SEN and yet still weave through the contemporary aspects of the field.

The second grouping of concepts relates to definitions and terminology. SEN is replete with debate and controversy regarding what is (or is not) an appropriate term to describe individual differences in learning. Some commentators, referring to this, have used the term 'balkanisation' to describe recent SEN provision, in that categories and groupings of children and young people seem to be increasing rapidly in the modern era, with new 'syndromes' (together with interest groups and advocates to promote them) being highlighted on a regular basis. This brings with it huge and challenging questions regarding equity and labelling, amongst other things.

A cluster of concepts relating to recent legislation and official policy and guidance comprise the next section of the book. It will be readily apparent that the modern era (which, for the purposes of this book, is viewed as being from 1978 onwards) has witnessed intense activity in legislation and official guidance in SEN. Much of this has been underpinned by a set of explicit philosophical principles, whilst also being driven by the influence of interest groups and key stakeholders.

Fourth, the book provides a set of concepts which address those aspects of current provision and practice which are the product of the legislative endeavour. Here there is consideration of such issues as mainstream or special-school provision, the taught curriculum and how it is made accessible to those with SEN, as well as a range of topics relating to learning and teaching.

The final set of key concepts considers the role of the principal stakeholders in SEN: pupils, professionals and parents. Perhaps nowhere is the complex nature of SEN better illustrated than an examination of the rapid rise in the numbers of professionals who are involved in working in this area. SEN, in its earliest historical form, was the preserve of medical doctors and then psychologists. Now, as a result of several decades of developing interdisciplinary collaboration, work in this area is undertaken by a significant and diverse range of professionals. Furthermore, recognition of the rights of children and young people as stakeholders, as well as the integral role of parents, has resulted in the incorporation of them in planning and decision making in all matters relating to their education, health and social welfare.

At the start of this introduction I stated that there was no intention to attempt a comprehensive coverage of every concept, idea or practice that has been utilised in SEN. Similarly, readers will need to view each of the concepts chosen with some caution. Each is certainly an important aspect of contemporary activity in the field, and the collection of concepts has, in a sense, been validated by a reference group of stakeholders. But the descriptions and commentaries themselves are only an outline introduction to each individual concept – that is really all they can be in a volume of this size. Nevertheless it is hoped that what is offered under each heading provides a tantalising glimpse into what is an exciting yet demanding element of education and wider society. And that this brief set of *concepti* will be the impetus for readers to explore SEN in even greater depth and, hopefully for some, to become practically involved in this challenging but always rewarding aspect of education.

HISTORICAL DIMENSIONS AND CURRENT THEMES

ABILITY AND ATTAINMENT

The term ability usually refers to a pupil's potential for success in school. Attainment, on the other hand, relates to what a child has actually learned. Both terms have been widely used in general education, and their implications for SEN are significant.

Traditional forms of **assessment** in education have been tests to 'measure' ability (an intelligence quotient (IQ) test is a good example of this) or attainment (as in the case of a test of a pupil's level of reading). Historically, both approaches were widely applied as a tool to identify pupils who needed remedial help. Unfortunately, measures of ability can imply that this is something that is fixed in a child, and not amenable to development over time. Moreover, there is a presupposition that intelligence can be measured, and that such 'tests' are culturally fair.

Similarly with attainment scores: these have been used to determine the level of performance of a given skill. Whilst this can be a useful means of gathering baseline performance data (in order, for example, to accurately target a lesson to meet the capability of pupils), it also can be a highly problematic issue. Many attainment tests are norm referenced, so that one child can easily be compared with the next. For instance, reading tests are frequently norm referenced, so that a child's performance is expressed as a reading age, thus making comparison with other pupils straightforward. Both ability and attainment tests have been used throughout the development of SEN by **educational psychologists**, and have come to be regarded as a quantitative measure of performance. In reality, however, such approaches assessed only a small element of a child's overall functioning.

Nevertheless, the **Education 'Reform' Act 1988** introduced standard attainment tests (SATs) so that all children could be compared across all national curriculum subjects. This, like the widespread application of ability and attainment tests before it, had major implications for pupils with SEN.

One way in which such tests have had an impact is their use as devices to sift and sort groups by performance in a limited range of aspects of learning. Little attention has been given to alternative ways in which ability and attainment can be quantified, so that learners who have skills and aptitudes in areas outside a relatively narrow set of test items might be deemed as underachieving, or as having an SEN.

Discussion point/question: To what degree is the term 'ability' located predominantly in traditional, socially acceptable interpretations

3

of the term? In an era of individualised learning, should not pupils be assessed as 'differently able'?

Further reading

Woolfson, L. and Grant, E. (2005) 'A comparison of special, regular and support teachers' beliefs about children's learning difficulties.' International Special Education Conference, 1–4 August, Strathclyde University.

See also: assessment

ADVOCACY AND EMPOWERMENT

This is a term which refers to the process of speaking and/or acting on behalf of pupils with SEN in order that their interests are promoted and their rights are preserved. The process includes advocating on behalf of parents of pupils with SEN, some of whom find the statutory procedures and the bureaucracy that comes with them quite bewildering. It should not be forgotten, however, that parents of pupils with SEN are often their fiercest advocates. The term is also linked closely with self-advocacy, in which a disabled person actively seeks to protect their rights and interests.

The role of the SEN advocate first came into prominence in the 1970s, notably in the USA. Here charitable organisations and volunteers sought to campaign on behalf of children with SEN and their families. This has traditionally been done in a number of ways. Such advocates (whether groups or individuals) sought to bring pressure on governments to seek changes in policy or improvements in provision and resources. At a more local, school-based level they would act directly on behalf of an individual pupil in cases, for example, where a pupil has been excluded from school or when a parent's request for a place for their child in a particular school is not being met.

The emergence of international awareness regarding the rights of children (illustrated for example by the **United Nations Convention on the Rights of the Child (1989)**) prompted wider developments in advocacy mechanisms in many countries.

The growth of advocacy in England has closely paralleled these developments. The inclusion of the views of parents and pupils in decision making about education, was highlighted in the **Warnock Report (1978)**, heralding the advent of a period of unprecedented growth in advocacy and self-advocacy. The **Education Act 1981**, and subsequent educational legislation, made advocacy an imperative element of policy. In consequence, the subsequent period leading to the present day, has seen a remarkable emphasis on advocacy and self-advocacy, which have their manifestations in the practical ways in which SEN pupils are educated. Indeed, the 1981 Act introduced the notion of 'appeals', whereby parents or other advocates had the right to appeal directly to the Secretary of State in cases where a '**statement of SEN**' was not deemed to be necessary, or where the content of a 'statement' was regarded by parents to be inadequate.

A number of examples can serve to illustrate the trend. In schools, it is now a requirement that parents and pupils are actively involved in periodic reviews of pupil progress. The **Code of Practice (2001)** spells out this requirement, and provides advice to both teachers and parents as to how this can be operationalised. For instance, parents and pupils should have a 'voice' in reviews of individual education plans, whilst their involvement in annual reviews is again an explicit requirement in the Code.

Another level in which the process of advocacy is apparent is in relation to the advocacy structures that have been put in place to ensure that any queries or disagreements can be resolved. The Special Educational Needs and Disability Tribunal was set up by the Education Act 1993 to consider parents' appeals against the decisions of **local authorities** (LAs) about children's SEN if parents cannot reach agreement with the LA. The **SEN Tribunal** is independent and its members are appointed by the Secretary of State for Children, Schools and Families. The Government cannot influence the Tribunal's decision, and the Tribunal has no connection with any LA. Two teams are responsible for appeals in each LA, and since 1994 the Tribunal has dealt with over 34000 cases. Over 3000 separate appeals were registered in 2006/7 alone.

Many other non-statutory and charitable groups have emerged as leading advocates for pupils with SEN. Whilst these have always played a major role in defending the rights of those with SEN and disabilities, the impact of statutory guidance on schools and LAs has made their position much stronger and their influence arguably greater.

Discussion point/question: What are the advantages and disadvantages of enabling children and young people who experience learning difficulties to make decisions regarding their own education?

Further reading

Garner, P. and Sandow, S. (eds) (1996) *Advocacy, Self-Advocacy and Special Needs*. London: David Fulton.

See also: children's rights; Code of Practice

CHILD PROTECTION

Child protection is the generic term to describe philosophies, policies, standards, guidelines and procedures to protect children from both intentional and unintentional harm. In the current context, it applies especially to the responsibilities placed on educational settings and those who work within them for the children and young people in their care. The term has become widely used beyond this definition, however, and is now also applied to the wider community or social environment. This can lead to confusion when discussing the child-protection responsibilities, as the term does have important implications for other sets of professionals: for example, both social workers and police are involved in cases where domestic violence occurs or when there is sexual exploitation of children.

There are four broad categories into which child-protection issues can be considered. For schools, one of the most visible is peer abuse, commonly referred to as bullying. This can be physical or psychological, and sometimes both. Moreover, the term is taken also to mean sexual abuse and gang violence. Schools are now required to set out how they prevent bullying: this is normally done in the form of a whole-school policy.

A second grouping relates to domestic violence. Again, this can be both physical and psychological, and the term is also taken to refer to sexual abuse. The current legislation and the emphasis on inter-disciplinary work by child-protection teams is the direct result of a number of very high-profile cases of horrific abuse of children, in which the victim's plight has gone unnoticed by professional groups working in isolation.

Third, the concept of societal abuse needs to be considered. This covers a wide range of concerns, some of which have complex cultural underpinnings. For example, some religions can condone physical punishment or humiliation of children as an acceptable child-rearing practice. Culturally, traditional practices such as female genital mutilation or scarification would also fall into this category. Equally important in this group is the high incidence of violent images in various media formats (film, television, electronic gaming and so on), as well as the promotion of negative attitudes towards children as the 'goods and chattels' of adults.

A final category relates to those children who engage in self-harming behaviour. This includes deliberately cutting or harming, suicidal thoughts, and attempted and actual suicide.

What has become widely known is that abuse and violence against children may be perpetrated by anyone, irrespective of their status or association with the child. Those working directly with children (teachers, social workers, house parents, volunteers and so on) have to follow strict procedures to ensure that they remain professionally distanced yet engaged with the children they work with. Equally, it is also widely understood that most abuse of children (and especially in cases of sexual abuse) occurs within either the family or extended family or a community friendship group.

Official responses to these cases have been a high priority, especially so from the publicity given to such cases as that of Jasmine Beckford, Victoria Climbie and the Soham murders. Such responses are ongoing, as witnessed in November 2008 by the 'Baby P' case in Haringey, North London.

Most schools now have robust child-protection policies. This provides a framework of principles, standards and guidelines on which to base individual and organisational practice in relation to creating a safe and 'child-friendly' environment. Schools are especially conscious of the official guidance and their legal responsibilities in this area, given the nature of their work.

Discussion point/question: Are some children who experience SEN more likely to be in need of child-protection measures than other children? Do you think that there has been any increase, over the years, in the incidences of child abuse?

Further reading

Baginsky, M. (2002) *Child Protection and Education*, NSPCC Research Briefing. London: NSPCC.

See also: Children Act; Every Child Matters; team around the child; bullying

CHILDREN'S RIGHTS

Children have a right to be protected under both domestic and international law. This means that there is a requirement to ensure that they are free from harm and that their basic physical and social needs are to be met. Traditional approaches with children in education were based on the uncompromisingly old-fashioned view that children should be 'seen and not heard'. As such, children were not regarded as active contributors to their own learning. They had very little direct involvement or say in what decisions were made on their behalf. But there has been a significant shift in attitude toward children's rights in education in the past 15 or so years. This change has coincided with the passing of important international and national legislation, including the **United Nations Convention on the Rights of the Child 1989** and the **Children Act 1989**. Article 12 of the UN Convention, for example, requires that children's views must be sought and given due weight in all matters affecting them. These various legislative measures provided the impetus to a shift from a welfare-oriented approach, which focused mainly on children's basic welfare needs, to the more recent position in which children are encouraged to express their views and participate in educational decision making.

One issue of some debate relates to the rather flexible legal definition of childhood. Thus, children do not acquire full legal independence until they reach the age of 18, but the law is somewhat inconsistent in that children can legally engage in certain adult activities before that age, including joining the armed forces at the age of 16. Moreover, there is a wide range of maturation across any group of children. Some will be far less able to make informed decisions at 14 or 15 years than others, irrespective of whether the pupil has an SEN.

In 2003 the UK government appointed the first Minister for Children, Young People and Families, following a recommendation contained in the UN Convention. Subsequently, major policy initiatives were introduced, including a green paper pointedly entitled **Every Child Matters**. Moreover, a new post of Children's Commissioner for England was established. All these initiatives signal a shift away from the child as a passive object, or the chattel of a parent.

Discussion point/question: What is the range of opportunities that children have to participate in making decisions about their own education? Should a child with SEN be viewed as a 'special case'?

Further reading

Kenworthy, J. and Whittaker, J. (2000) 'Anything to declare? The struggle for inclusive education and children's rights', *Disability and Society*, 15(2), 219–31.

See also: Children Act; Every Child Matters; Team around the child

COGNITIVE DEVELOPMENT

The development over time of a child's intellect is usually referred to as cognitive development. Whilst a school does have guidance and recreational roles, its principal task is to assist in the growth of pupils' cognitive skills. The importance of cognitive development to SEN is central in that an inability to function in the cognitive domain is fundamentally linked to learning difficulties.

The concept subsumes a number of theoretical explanations, all of which have a degree of currency. Piagetian theory is based on the notion that children develop levels of cognitive capacity and that, in consequence, teaching has to be pitched at an appropriate level for children to learn. Whilst such an approach has widespread currency in general education, its application in SEN teaching and **assessment** has been immensely influential.

Another explanation relates to social activity theory. Here one view is that children learn by having a particular skill demonstrated or modelled. They take clues from this, and, with continued reinforcement through modelling, gradually enhance their cognitive ability in that area of skill. Again, the approach is a frequently used SEN intervention strategy.

Behavioural psychologists adopt a further position. They would argue that cognitive skills are best learned using reinforcement and rewards. But it is important to recognise that cognitive growth is not necessarily incremental, nor does it follow a continuously rising continuum of progression.

Discussion point/question: Is a child's cognitive development influenced by environment? Can children be 'taught' cognitive skills?

Further reading

Child, D. (2005) 'Concept formation and cognitive development', in S. Child *Psychology and the Teacher*. London: Continuum, 61–88.

See also: assessment

CONTROVERSIAL ISSUES

SEN itself has, in many respects, been a controversial issue in general education for a very long time. Debates range consistently regarding our beliefs and suppositions about 'handicap', the use of terminology, the nature of specific SEN, the type of educational provision for children and major questions regarding resources. Many of these controversial aspects are referred to elsewhere in this collection of concepts. It is important to recognise the contested nature of many of these, and the policy decisions made regarding them have huge implications for the key stakeholders of SEN (the children and young people and their parents or carers). They can, in various ways, create false hope of a 'cure', they can become commercialised, and they can lead to the generation of a kind of educational fundamentalism, a unilateral belief and commitment to a given explanation or strategy at the expense of all others.

A useful summary of the range of controversies, although by no means an exhaustive account, is provided by Hornby, Atkinson and Howard (1997). They identify a number of groups of issues which have caused continuous professional and sometimes public debate over the last ten or so years. These authors firstly consider controversial diagnoses, where there is considerable scientific debate regarding the causes and aetiology of particular syndromes. In some cases, too, there are suggestions that the 'syndrome' being proposed is a social construct. Typical of the controversial diagnoses in SEN are such disabilities as **autism**, **dyslexia** and **attention deficit disorders**, although several others (for example, **emotional and behavioural difficulties**) could be added.

A second grouping considers what are frequently referred to as 'systemic interventions'. These are those policies and actions which are applied throughout the school system to address SEN. The quintessential example, which has become an enduring debate amongst educational practitioners as well as parents and policy makers, is the issue of **inclusion** versus separate schooling. Even politicians are regularly embroiled in this debate, so contentious and polarised has it become. Another generic issue in SEN, related to a very large extent, is the question of **exclusion**. In this case, questions are rightly asked about whose needs are being met when schools exclude young people on account of their challenging behaviour.

SEN practice has been characterised by teaching approaches which often have widespread validation from professionals; these might include differentiation and individual education plans. Even these, though, carry with them an element of controversy. But there are some strategies which have invoked quite passionate debate amongst a wide range of stakeholders. These include such interventions as conductive education, instrumental enrichment, and the so-called 'Dore method', described variously as a 'miracle cure for dyslexia'.

One of the important impacts of the popular discussion of any of these controversial issues is that media dramatisation and overstatement sometimes takes over what was perhaps (in some cases) a legitimate but small-scale experimental finding. Given that parents of children who have SEN and disabilities, as well as teachers and others professionally involved with them, are most usually wholly committed to exploring every conceivable opportunity to make positive progress in addressing SEN, they can sometimes be influenced by such overstatements. This is not to be critical of teachers or parents: sometimes recommendations regarding the efficacy of a supposedly 'proven' policy, diagnosis or intervention can come from authoritative sources (for example, government advisers, eminent researchers or national icons). This can be very persuasive at a time when all concerned are endeavouring to find ways of dealing with SEN.

Discussion point/question: Are there any current controversies which you know of which impact on children and young people with SEN?

Further reading

Hornby, G., Atkinson, M. and Howard, J. (1997) *Controversial Issues in Special Education*. London: David Fulton.

See also: categories of SEN

DELINQUENCY

Children who behave in an antisocial way (for example, stealing, rowdy public behaviour including aggression to others, some motor vehicle offences) which results in a criminal offence being committed are referred to as 'delinquents'. The term commonly used as a collective descriptor for their actions is 'delinquency'. It has been used for many years in both education and the social sciences and is also now synonymous with terms such as 'youth crime', although popular usage has seen the expression 'delinquent' applied to a wide variety of non-criminal actions. In strict terms, though, 'delinquency' relates expressly to those actions by children and young people which result in their being charged with an offence which is subsequently dealt with by the juvenile courts.

In terms of broad characteristics, delinquent activity amongst younger children tends to be characterised by petty theft or truancy from school. Older pupils are more likely to engage in aggressive behaviour in addition to other antisocial acts. There is traditionally a much larger proportion of boys than girls implicated in delinquent behaviours which results in their being dealt with by the youth justice system.

Its relationship to SEN is substantial. At a public level there is a traditional association with standards of behaviour in public social spaces and the social skills taught (at least in part) in schools. The perceived decline in standards of public behaviour amongst young people is associated by some with declining standards of 'discipline' in schools. This linkage has been made more substantive in recent years with the growth of the so-called 'citizenship' agenda, which seeks to inculcate a set of responsibilities in young people. Schools are seen as the principal setting in which this agenda is delivered. Certain pupils have difficulties, for a variety of reasons, in connecting with this area of work. There will frequently be an overlap between problem behaviour in school and antisocial (delinquent) behaviour outside it. Indeed, the two aspects are largely synonymous in the way that some adolescents function socially. Pupils who experience **emotional and behavioural difficulties** are most commonly implicated.

There are many theories of delinquency. Each shows a level of overlap with the explanations given for emotional and behavioural difficulties. They include genetic factors, poverty, alienation from school and anomie (an inability to gain success through accepted social pathways – for example, examination success, sporting achievement). Environmental factors relating to families and upbringing have also been invoked as explanations, whilst the human need to belong to groups is viewed as a possible factor in accounting for delinquent gangs.

Discussion point/question: Do pupils who frequently present behaviour problems within schools automatically become involved in antisocial behaviour outside it? Which, in your opinion, comes first?

Further reading

Sprague, J., Walker, H., Stieber, S., Simonsen, B., Nishioka, V. and Wagner, L. (2001) 'Exploring the relationship between school discipline referrals and delinquency', *Psychology in the Schools*, 38(2), 197–206.

See also: emotional and behavioural difficulties

DEVIANCE

Deviance is a concept which is an essential underpinning theme when considering pupil behaviour in its widest sense. In consequence it has importance for SEN in that theories of deviance can help to shed light on both the problematic behaviour of pupils and, equally importantly, educational responses to them. The term refers to the motivated tendency of an individual to contravene a norm. As such it is an expression which refers to social interaction.

One of the significant efforts in the sociology of deviance has been the task of examining the term in relation to what constitutes **normality**. This is of particular interest in schools, which are social organisations with sets of rules, protocols and procedures. Given that each of these varies from one school to the next, a deviant act needs to be located as much in 'place' as anything else. For instance, a refusal to adhere to a school's policy on pupil uniform may be taken as a 'deviant' act; but it can only be described thus in that setting (it may well not be 'deviant' in a school that does not have a formal policy on uniform). Similar analogies can be made regarding many other pupil behaviours. Given that pupil 'behaviour' is essentially norm referenced, this has important implications for the way that pupils are viewed, and especially those whose 'deviance' leads them to be referred to as having a 'behaviour difficulty'.

Discussion point/question: Is the term 'deviant' a useful one in the context of children and young people who behave inappropriately in school? Should its use be related to sociological, rather than educational, discussion?

Further reading

Waterhouse, S. (2004) 'Deviant and non-deviant identities in the classroom: Patrolling the boundaries of the normal social world', *European Journal of Special Needs Education*, 19(1), 1–15.

See also: delinquency; normality and difference

DISADVANTAGE

Whilst it was not until the Second World War that the deprivation experienced by many children in inner cities and towns became apparent, there have been numerous historical accounts documenting the lives of the urban poor. One famous example of this literature is the account of London's poorest communities by Booth (1902), whilst social reformers like Joseph Rowntree around the same time were driven to respond to the plight of the 'victims' of industrialisation. Subsequently, many researchers and social theorists have used evidence bases to demonstrate the close linkage between disadvantaging factors in society and the educational performance of children and young people.

Essen and Wedge (1982) used longitudinal data from the National Child Development Study to show the link between underachievement and such disadvantage indicators as poor housing, single-parent families and low income. Prior to this there was a tendency to look only at the pupil for an explanation of learning failure. The links between SEN and poverty and **disadvantage** have been reinforced by other, more recent work and has in part been responsible for influencing policy change in this area. One example of this has been the establishment of 'education action zones' by the New Labour government (later to become part of the **Excellence in Cities** initiative), which were intended to address social and educational shortcomings in a number of specific urban settings. Many argued that such an approach simply demonstrated the intractability of the problem, given that broadly similar initiatives have been invoked in similar locations over 30 years previously.

Discussion point/question: Is poverty, poor housing or unemployment simply an excuse for the failure of some pupils to achieve or behave appropriately in school?

Further reading

Dyson, A. (1997) 'Social and educational disadvantage: Reconnecting special needs education', *British Journal of Special Education*, 24(4), 152–7.

See also: social class; Excellence in Cities

DISRUPTIVE BEHAVIOUR

A term which carried significance particularly during the 1970s and 1980s, the expression 'disruptive behaviour' became, during that time, a quasi-official term for those behaviours which were deemed to be contrary to the accepted norms within a school. The term was also sometimes taken as being synonymous with 'disruptive pupils', although a focus on behaviour meant that variations in behaviour (from one lesson to the next, at different times in the school day, with different teachers or groups of pupils) were the focus of attention rather than the pupil. During the 1970s a large number of local education authorities established 'disruptive units', these being settings where pupils whose behaviour was consistently problematic in **mainstream schools** were educated.

'Disruptive behaviour' as a term has come to be seen as problematic for a number of reasons. First, the term, whilst it purports to describe a pupil's behaviour, in a given situation is not specific enough to be helpful. If a pupil is said to have engaged in 'disruptive behaviour' this can refer to anything from unwanted talking during a lesson, to continuously moving around a classroom without permission and, at the other extreme, verbally or physically aggressive behaviour to a teacher or peer. The lack of specificity, inherent in the term, means that a targeted intervention cannot be planned.

Second, there is the assumption that disruptive behaviour automatically refers to violent or aggressive 'acting-out' behaviour. This impression is often fuelled by media portrayals of pupils and schools. Only the most extreme incidents of school disruption are nationally reported; for instance, whereas teachers report that less obvious problem behaviour (including the so-called 'low-level' problem behaviour like talking out of turn, failure to arrive at a lesson on time) is far more common and yet usually escapes media attention.

Third, the term tends to place causal emphasis on the pupil. In other words, complex underlying issues such as the place where the behaviour occurs and the role of others in influencing the behaviour are less obviously taken account of. Indeed, the widespread use of the expression 'disruptive pupils' in the 1970s and 1980s is a manifestation of an assumption that the principal determinant of the behaviour is the pupil.

The term 'disruptive behaviour' has, in fact, come to be regarded as a catch-all term for the unwanted problem behaviour of pupils in schools. Its practical use, however, has been questioned in recent years and the term tends not to be used as widely as hitherto.

Discussion point/question: Compare your own definition of 'disruptive behaviour' with that of a fellow student or colleague. What are the similarities and differences?

Further reading

Kaplan A., Gheen M. and Midgley, C. (2002) 'Classroom goal structure and student disruptive behaviour', *British Journal of Educational Psychology*, 72(2), 191–211.

See also: emotional and behavioural difficulties; exclusion

EARLY SEN LEGISLATION

The emergence of 'special education' in England (and the rest of the UK) is a relatively recent phenomenon. The accompanying legislation is, similarly, of quite recent origin, and what follows comprises some indicative examples of the thinking and attendant terminology of these early attempts to legislate for a significant minority of the population. Whilst the Forster Education Act (1870), which established school boards in England to provide an elementary education in certain areas, did not include disabled children in its provision, the London School Board had established a special class for the deaf in 1874. Even earlier, in Scotland, the Lunacy (Scotland) Act of 1862 authorised the granting of licences to charitable institutions for the care and training of 'imbecile children'.

The Royal Commission on the Blind and Deaf reported in 1889. It recommended compulsory education for the blind from 5 to 16, either provided by school boards or in institutions run by others. Similar recommendations were made for the deaf, but given that these children were viewed to be less well advanced in their learning, they would be educated separately and not begin schooling until they were aged seven. These recommendations were enshrined in the Elementary Education (Blind and Deaf Children) Act of 1893.

Little attention was directed towards children with a mental handicap at this time, although the Royal Commission did distinguish between children who were termed 'feeble minded', 'imbeciles' and 'idiots'. Subsequently, in 1896, the Education Department established a Committee on Defective and Epileptic Children, which determined that school authorities needed to make provision for all defective children in their area. The Elementary (Defective and Epileptic) Act of 1914 made it the legal responsibility of school authorities to attend to the education of 'mentally defective children'.

The education of 'mentally defective' children was the focus of the 1924 Mental Deficiency Committee. The work of this committee is interesting, in that for virtually the first time there was an indication of the growth of a belief that those children who were regarded as having a 'mental deficiency' should not necessarily be separated from those in mainstream education – a line of argument which, however crudely developed, was in fact years ahead of its time. Nevertheless, in spite of these hopeful signs, some 40 or more years were to elapse before children with a mental handicap were automatically entitled to an education.

Discussion point/question: Why do you think that emphasis in legislation was first directed towards children who were deaf or blind? Is there a common-sense explanation?

Further reading

Sutherland, G. (1981) 'The origins of special education', in W. Swann (ed.) *The Practice of Special Education*. Oxford: Blackwell/Open University Press, 93–101.

See also: importance of history; SEN in history; historical 'language' of SEN; models of SEN

EXCLUSION

When the behaviour of a child or young person becomes consistently unacceptable, or when a single incident occurs in which the behaviour of the pupil is regarded as a serious breach of the school's accepted policy, a decision can be taken to exclude. This action constitutes the ultimate school-based response to misconduct. There are two forms of exclusion – fixed term and permanent. In the case of the former, the head teacher is required to inform the school's governing body if a pupil is being excluded for more than 15 days in any one term. Moreover, although pupils can be excluded for one or more fixed-term periods, this may not exceed 45 school days in any one school year.

The exclusion of pupils who present behaviour problems has been viewed as a growing national concern. In spite of this, the data evidence for this is inconclusive, with numbers of pupils excluded in primary and secondary schools remaining consistently around 12,000 per annum. At one level of analysis this might seem a high figure. But when it is recognised that there are over 25,000 schools in England, catering for a school age population of 8,149,200 (DfES 2006/7), the figure is not high from the perspective of statistical significance.

From September 2007 schools have been required to arrange full-time education for any pupils excluded for a fixed period from the sixth day of exclusion, and local authorities likewise from the sixth day of a permanent exclusion. Prior to any exclusion taking place, the school must take all reasonable steps to ensure that the parents of the excluded child are notified, ideally by telephone on the day of the exclusion and also informed in writing.

There is an over-representation of children and young people who have SEN in the number of excluded pupils from primary and secondary schools in England. As the majority of exclusions are on account of persistent unacceptable behaviour, this is consistent with the established correlation between **emotional and behavioural difficulties** and SEN.

Discussion point/question: What is your view regarding the relative importance of factors which lead to a pupil being excluded from school? Why do more exclusions occur in secondary, rather than primary, school?

Further reading

Parsons, D., Hayden, C., Godfrey, R., Howlett, K. and Martin, T. (2002) *Outcomes in Secondary Education for Children Excluded from Primary School*, Research Report 271. London: DfES.

See also: emotional and behavioural difficulties; disruptive behaviour

GENDER DIFFERENCES

There has been consistent media attention directed towards the underperformance of boys in school. They appear to perform less well than girls across many curriculum areas, and especially so in maths and English. What is less well known, certainly by the general public, is that boys outnumber girls in virtually every category of SEN. This figure also subsumes some dramatic gender imbalances. For example, in the area of reading difficulties boys outnumber girls by 10 to 1, whilst a similar high discrepancy can be noted amongst pupils presenting **emotional and behavioural difficulties**. The ratio is more equable between boys and girls in cases of severe SEN.

A number of explanations have been given for these imbalances. Some have advanced the argument that physiologically the male is more susceptible to damage, whilst others suggest that boys are less likely to conform to rules, thus making them more at risk of being involved in cases of disobedience resulting in sanctions than school **exclusion**. Others have explored psychological differences and those of socialised roles as a key to understanding the ongoing imbalance between boys and girls in the data on SEN. And there have been an increasing number of researchers and theorists who have regarded the absence of positive male role models to be implicated in boys' underachievement and over-representation in statistics regarding such issues as exclusion and emotional and behavioural difficulties.

Discussion point/question: Are gender imbalances in SEN made more visible by the way that learning and teaching is organised in schools?

Further reading

Daniels, H., Hey, V., Leonard, D. and Smith, M. (2000) 'Issues of equity in special needs education as seen from the perspective of gender', in H. Daniels (ed.) *Special Education Re-formed: Beyond Rhetoric?* London: Falmer Press, 47–66.

See also: emotional and behavioural difficulties; exclusion

GENETICS

Genes are the biochemical constituent which link a natural parent to their child – heredity. They are responsible for the transfer of characteristics or traits: half of the chromosomes in a newly fertilised organism are provided by the mother and half by the father. Several SEN are known to be linked to heredity, whilst considerable debate occurs about the possible genetic linkage in others. This connection also informs the '**nature and nurture**' discussion in SEN.

The scientific rationale for this parent–child transfer of a disability or SEN is straightforward: if both genes carry a disease then that disease will be inherited; if only one of the genes has a disease then it will depend entirely on whether it is the dominant gene or not. If it is dominant, then the disease will be inherited.

Historically many disabilities and SEN were attributed without question to genetic transfer. Indeed, such attribution did much to ensure the dominance of medical models of interpretation in the development of SEN. Moreover, this view ensured that SEN were 'illnesses' which were invariably not subject to amelioration or extinction other than by medicine. As a result early SEN was seen as the preserve of medical doctors and scientists.

Whilst the inheritability of many 'syndromes' or conditions has been scientifically demonstrated (for example, fragile-X syndrome or haemophilia) others are more contentious in their origins, and considerable debate occurs around their underlying cause. For example, there has been an ongoing discussion amongst scientists, researchers and educationists regarding the inheritability of **delinquent** or aggressive behaviour. Opinions are much divided, although in these cases there has been an emerging consensus that multifactorial cause is probably the explanation which is most tenable.

The prevalence of genetic transfer of disability has been greatly affected by genetic counselling, in which prospective parents are given informed advice concerning the likelihood that a particular disability might be transferred to their child. Scientific advances have meant that in some cases a fetus with a defective gene can be identified well in advance of the child's birth (as in the case of amniocentesis). This raises major ethical questions in the field of SEN and disability: at what level of likely 'disability' should parents, or the medical practitioners who advise them, decide that a pregnancy should be terminated? This issue needs also to be linked to the natural desire of all parents to have healthy children.

Discussion point/question: Morality and science are said to clash headlong in the case of the hereditary transfer of disability. Do you think this is an accurate summation?

Further reading

Shakespeare, T. (1998) 'Choices and rights: Eugenics, genetics and disability equality', *Disability and Society*, 13(5), 665–81.

See also: nature and nurture; delinquent

HISTORICAL 'LANGUAGE' OF SEN

A study of the history of SEN will illustrate its gradual shift away from the use of medical language to describe learning difficulties. In doing so the terms that have historically been utilised in reference to what are known as 'pupils with SEN' can be highlighted as being often pejorative or deficit laden, and nearly always negative. Many of the terms used by professionals over the last 200 years were subsequently used in common parlance to describe inadequate, physically unattractive or delinquent individuals in day-to-day life. Terms such as 'backward', 'retarded', 'educationally subnormal', or 'feeble minded' were used in official policy and legislation less than 100 years ago.

Others, such as 'remedial' and 'maladjusted' have an even more recent currency. Both are illustrative of the rapid shift that has taken place in education in terms of professional knowledge and practices towards pupils with SEN. In the first case, the term 'remedial teaching' comprised the provision of special help to those children who experienced reading problems and were referred to as 'retarded'. This assistance was provided in ordinary (mainstream) schools, originally by peripatetic (i.e. visiting) teachers. Later the term was extended to incorporate all additional curriculum support, and so-called 'remedial departments' became widespread in ordinary schools. The advent of the move towards integration during the 1970s saw the replacement of remedial provision by 'support teaching'.

The second illustrative term, 'maladjusted', is equally contentious and revealing of a particular negative and blame-allocating view of pupil behaviour. It was used up until the 1970s, and implied that the causes for unwanted problem behaviour were entirely located within the child. In other words, there was little or no recognition that other causal factors, such as the impact of schools, social relationships or other external issues might have some part to play.

Discussion point/question: Recollecting your own days in school, do you recall any pejorative names being used to describe children who would today be termed as having SEN? What were your feelings then … and now?

Further reading

Corbett, J. (1996) *Bad Mouthing: The Language of Special Needs.* London: Falmer Press.

See also: early SEN legislation; SEN in history; historical 'language' of SEN; models of SEN

IMPORTANCE OF HISTORY

Physicians and psychologists have been dominant gatekeepers within SEN for almost a hundred years. Prior to this the organised churches played a central role in caring for, rather than educating, those who today would be viewed as having SEN. In the case of the medical profession, the first formal responses to SEN in England came from doctors, usually working for charity groups. Their preoccupation was first with identifiable physical handicaps. Thus, in 1838, the London Society for Teaching the Blind to Read opened schools, first in London, then Nottingham and Exeter. The Egerton Commission (1889) was dominated by physicians, and set out recommendations for the compulsory education of blind children, deaf children and also for children who were seen as mentally handicapped – the Commission identified three groupings: 'idiots', 'imbeciles' and the 'feeble minded'. It argued that the latter two were educable, and provision in separate **special schools** was recommended.

These earliest events, signalling society's preoccupation with clinical diagnosis, leading to specific educational outcomes for children with SEN, set the scene on what was to follow throughout (according to some commentators) the twentieth century. The influence of both physicians and **educational psychologists** has remained through to the present day. Indeed, it is fair to suggest that both professions have had a pervasive gate-keeping role throughout the entire history of SEN. Understanding the nature of inter-professional collaboration in the twenty-first century is greatly assisted by recognising the power that clinicians have, especially in making 'judgements' about what is (or is not) a 'normal' level of social or educational functioning.

Discussion point/question: Consider your own time at school: to what extent did your involvement with children who were in some way 'different' inform your subsequent thinking about SEN and disability?

Further reading

Potts, P. (1995) 'What's the use of history? Understanding educational provision for disabled students and those who experience difficulties in learning', *British Journal of Educational Studies*, 43(4), 398–411.

See also: early SEN legislation; historical 'language' of SEN; models of SEN

INCLUSION AND INDIVIDUAL RIGHTS

The concept and practice of educational inclusion has become the prevailing initiative in education systems throughout Western Europe, and elsewhere. It has been driven by a laudable commitment to the rights of all learners to secure the opportunities to enable them to function as equal participants in twenty-first century society. In special education, the growth of interest in inclusion has been land-marked by a number of key events in the past ten or so years. Not least amongst these was the **Salamanca Statement (1994)**, which stated that 'every child has a fundamental right to education and must be given the opportunity to achieve and maintain acceptable levels of learning' (UNESCO, 1994).

So, at the outset, inclusive practice has been predicated by a moral position based on a recognition of individual rights. In the last few years increasing importance has been placed on this principle by national and local governments. A significant number of academics, administrators, politicians, parents and practitioners have come to regard the approach as the single most effective means of 'combating discriminatory attitudes, creating welcoming communities, building an inclusive society and achieving education for all' (UNESCO, 1994).

At the same time, however, the preoccupation with the moral argument for inclusion has deflected the need to advance a set of clear arguments which can be used to justify a unilateral, wholesale adoption of inclusive practice in education. Up until the present time there has been little need to provide such justification, as policy makers and practitioners have been swept along on a tidal wave of 'feel-good' as a consequence of buoyant economies and a new political order. In consequence, educational inclusion, in its infant phase, has been largely populated by fundamentalists, who have presented a highly polarised – even pejorative – version. This regards full inclusionists as inhabiting a special place of grace, a morally superior standpoint, compared with those who, as Sowell (1995) points out, are categorised as the 'benighted' – the cynics who need time to adjust to the changing order of things. Others have viewed this polarity in even more forthright terms: 'Some full inclusionists talk as though they are in a battle pitting the forces of morality against the forces of immorality' (Shanker, 1994).

Latterly, therefore, there has been a tendency to look beyond a simplistic connection between inclusion and the rights of pupils with SEN. There has been recognition that the term 'inclusion' is a very problematic one. Some have argued, for example, that separate settings can, in many respects, be viewed as protecting the 'rights' of individual pupils (and/or the wishes of their parents) by ensuring that access is provided to an education which is appropriate to their needs and which will subsequently enable pupils to successfully achieve the transition from school into wider society.

Discussion point/question: Is the inclusion of all learners within mainstream schools an automatic human right, or should other factors be taken into account?

Further reading

Florian, L., Rouse, M. and Black Hawkins, K. (2007) *Achievement and Inclusion in Schools*. London: Routledge.

See also: integration; advocacy and empowerment

INTEGRATION

The concept of integration is located in a view that pupils with SEN should be educated alongside the rest of the school population and enjoy all the benefits that follow from this. In some national settings this process is referred to as 'mainstreaming' (for example, in the USA). In one sense it is useful to consider 'integration' as a broad educational principle which was the precursor of 'inclusion'. The debates surrounding the term are very similar to those which have overtaken the inclusion debate. But in all other respects any resemblance between the two, in terms of their underpinning orientation, is at best tentative.

The origins of the term 'integration' in an English context date back over 25 years, and were heavily influenced by the progressive developments of Public Law 94–142, the Education for all Handicapped Children Act, which determined, amongst other things, that all children should be educated in the 'least restrictive practice', a term usually (although not exclusively) associated with mainstreaming. The **Warnock Report** and the subsequent **Education Act 1981** enshrined the concept in policy and guidance on practice.

The broad understanding and interpretation of the term was that there were three types of integration: locational (where pupils with SEN are educated on the same site as other pupils, but in separate 'units' or classrooms); social (where regular social integration takes place (for example mealtimes, playtime etc.) but the pupils are still educated separately; and functional (where pupils with SEN participate in regular classes and follow the same curriculum).

The 1981 Act required that integration of this kind should take place, providing it took account of the wishes of parents, and providing that it was educationally efficient and did not interfere with the education of others. This stance illustrates the sharp differences in philosophy between integration and **inclusion**. Integration, unlike inclusion, placed no particular emphasis on teachers, other adults, non-SEN pupils, and the culture and ethos of a school to change. The pupil with SEN had to 'fit in' to existing arrangements. The conditions placed on schools regarding 'efficient use of resources' meant that the spirit of the Act could easily be bypassed.

As has been implied, the concept of inclusion brought with it a considerable debate regarding the philosophy and efficacy of the approach. On the one hand, advocates of integration maintained that 'integration' was a moral right of all children, irrespective of need. They also claimed that many more children in mainstream settings would now be identified (and have their needs met) because of the additional attention and resources being directed towards mainstream schools. On the other hand, advocates of a separate special school system maintained that theirs was a realistic position because there would always be a need for **special schools** – a point made in the Warnock Report. Moreover, their view was that the needs of a small group of the most severely disabled pupils would always need specialist provision.

The argument between integration and separation has pre-dated that of inclusion versus specialist provision. That many of the justifications used on either side of the argument bear a close affinity to those being discussed at the present time regarding inclusion makes this issue one of the most enduring dilemmas and debates in education in the period subsequent to 1978.

Discussion point/question: How strongly could you argue for and against the concept of integration? Where do your own allegiances lie?

Further reading

Booth, T. (1988) 'Challenging conceptions of integration'. In Barton, L. (Ed.) *The Politics of Special Educational Needs*. London: Falmer Press, 97–122.

See also: integration; Warnock Report; Education Act 1981; inclusion and individual rights; special schools and settings

MODELS OF SEN

The history of special education has seen the emergence of a number of 'models', sets of concepts, ideas and practices which have been used to explain why some children, but not others, fail to thrive within the education system. Indeed, it is fair to say that when mention of 'models' of SEN is made in academic or professional circles, a wide range of views, sometimes polar in position, can surface.

Broadly, there are six core models used to explain the occurrence of, and response to, SEN. These can be summarised (in order of historical impact) as magical, moral medical, intellectual, social competence and social conspiracy models. Each, at various times in the history of SEN, has left in its wake a 'trail' which enables us to understand currently held beliefs and perceptions regarding this area of education.

The magical model is essentially pre-scientific, dating from the period before the Enlightenment in the latter part of the eighteenth century. This was a time when disability was seen as an act of God or, in other cases, an act of the Devil. As such 'disability' was seen to be beyond the control of individuals. The result of this was that people with squints, or harelips, or other physical deformities were seen as objects of fear. Even left-handedness was regarded as 'sinister'. This public perception was reinforced by the link between disability and 'evil' in literature and drama: witches in fairy tales, for example, were invariably portrayed as having physical deformities. Further, there was a link between disability and 'sin': prior to the Reformation, for example, there were relatively few days in the religious calendar when sexual intercourse was permitted – a disabled child could be seen as the result of 'excess' on the wrong day. Nor has the magical model been totally consigned to the past: recently an England soccer manager was dismissed for proposing that learning difficulties were the result of a spiritual visitation.

Historically, the moral model links disability and the individual responsibility of people to become as perfect as possible, a view which is informed by the underlying concept that all human beings are creatures of intent. Applied to those with disability or learning difficulty this is reduced to a belief that the person with a learning difficulty can do something to remedy the situation. Often too, this way of thinking equates a failure to learn with laziness. It is also interesting to link this orientation with the Poor Law of the nineteenth century, which viewed the 'undeserving poor' as being responsible for their own poverty because of fecklessness, alcohol or apathy.

The medical model was the dominant belief in the early development of SEN, and held the view that a 'difficulty' was present which was within the child or individual. It has remained a dominant model in SEN throughout most of the twentieth century. Any 'treatment' was mainly perceived to be the province of the medical profession, and the children or individuals were viewed more in need of hospitalisation, care and 'protection' than education. The dominant role of medicine informed and supported this model and promoted a negative image of disability. John Langdon Down (1866), for example, proposed an 'ethnic classification of idiocy' – including a group which now bears his name (whom he called 'Mongolian idiots'). Meanwhile, Morel (1857) identified a 'theory of degeneracy', in which he linked poverty and disability with generational abuse of alcohol and 'social corruption'.

The intellectual model was also informed by a powerful and emergent professional group whose views were closely linked to the determinism expressed by medical doctors of the day. It was based on intellectual determinism and is rooted in eugenics with regard to both ability and personality. The argument was that an individual's inheritance of intellectual performance was all powerful, and this would not subsequently be subject to change over time. This view, widely held in the late nineteenth century, found practical expression in the way that children were educated: the rich were capable of, and needed, a 'classical' education, while the poor did not. Towards the end of the nineteenth century this view was challenged as the mental-testing movement developed. During that time psychologists, using tests of intellectual capacity, became increasingly powerful, and joined medical doctors as a powerful group of decision makers in SEN. They acted as significant advisers to both national government and to local education services. Theirs was a view which maintained that children who experienced SEN did so on account of cognitive or emotional malfunction, mediated somewhat by the impact of environment (though such mediation tended mainly to be acknowledged in a later phase of the model's influence). The intellectual model has remained in evidence throughout the twentieth century – one example of this being the manner in which pupils are sifted and sorted in **National Curriculum** testing.

The social competence model proposes that an individual is accepted within society, based on the degree to which they are able to follow an agreed set of social rules or protocols. Built in to this way of thinking was the notion that educational establishments or other institutions could provide pupils with social skills and trades so that they could participate as 'useful' members of society. The so-called 'industrial schools' of the early twentieth century were examples of this. A social competence model also meant that those who were deemed incapable of following the conventions of society should be segregated for the protection and 'good' of the rest of society. The resulting establishment of 'asylums', usually situated in isolated locations in the countryside, was a material manifestation of this way of thinking.

A social conspiracy model is based on notions of normality and abnormality. What might be 'normal' in one context soon becomes abnormal in another. The analogy of apples and oranges illustrates the concept: in a basket of apples, all apples are, in appearance, normal. However, should one apple then be placed in a basket of oranges, it can be perceived as 'abnormal' (rather than different). The same argument can be applied to SEN. The very existence of social norms brings with it the need to establish ways of describing and quantifying those who do not fit within such norms. As a result of this there has been in the last fifty or so years a rapid increase in the number of identified 'handicaps', a movement which one author has referred to as the 'special needs industry'.

Discussion point/question: To what extent are the historical 'models' of SEN outlined above useful? Do they help you to understand contemporary provision?

Further reading

Sandow, S. (1994) *Whose Special Need?* London: Paul Chapman.

See also: normality and difference; SEN in history

NATURE AND NURTURE

The debate regarding nature versus nurture is long standing and has considerable importance in SEN. In summary, the polarities in the debate are centred around the impact on individual pupils of either heredity or environment. Crudely, it is a debate regarding whether or not a given person is 'born, not made' or vice versa.

Much of the existing work regarding the nature/nurture issue has been linked to intelligence (although the question of genetic transfer is a point of controversy across the field as a whole). This has had a massive impact on education in general and on SEN in particular.

The distinction between proponents of the opposing positions in the debate is sharply illustrated by the practical interventions that they inform. In England, the notion behind Sure Start is based on a principle that all children can achieve, irrespective of the underlying causes of educational failure. Children, irrespective of their social or physiological histories, can benefit from early intervention in their education. Adherents of this approach would mainly align themselves with the argument that environmental factors have the greatest impact on children's educational development.

A contrasting policy stance might be the preoccupation with so-called 'gifted children' or those with explicit aptitudes. These, it would be claimed, are inbuilt, a product of nature. Whilst they can be coached to perform at an even greater level of distinction, they can achieve only at this level because they have innate (mainly inherited) characteristics.

The polarisation of the debate has slowly been seen as unhelpful, however. As with many aspects of SEN provision and practice, a more holistic model appears to have gathered influence. Consequently, there is a view that whilst a very small percentage of pupils will have characteristics which will be expressed at a high level without external coaching, the majority of children possess physiological, cognitive and emotional qualities which, though at some level the product of a family trait, are necessarily wholly amenable to development and educational growth.

Discussion point/question: How has your family affected the course of your own education? Do your friends have an influence on what degree or vocational programme you decide to undertake?

Further reading

Deci, E., Vallerand, R., Pelletier, L. and Ryan, R. (1991) 'Motivation and education: The self-determination perspective', *Educational Psychologist*, 26 (3/4), 325–46.

See also: genetics; ability and attainment; disadvantage

NORMALITY AND DIFFERENCE

The concept of normality has been central to much of the traditional thinking and practice in SEN. At its heart is the negative perception that to be 'normal' is to be measured by the behaviours, performances and interactions of society as a whole. Whilst some interpretations of 'normalisation' link to the concept of equality, there has been a widely held but misguided belief that disabled people want to be 'normal' rather than as they are. This is described by some commentators as being one of the most oppressive experiences to which disabled people are subjected (Morris, 1993). It is argued, with a great deal of justification, that the quest to be 'normal' is simply reinforcing stereotypes of what comprises 'normality' at the expense of others who are 'different'. Again, Morris (1993) states that 'I do not want to have to try to emulate what a non-disabled woman looks like in order to assert positive things about myself. I want to be able to celebrate my difference, not hide from it.'

Normality is powerfully linked to social acceptance. A pupil is more likely to be included within the social and educational processes of a school if he or she is socially aware, knows the rules of engagement, succeeds in learning and does not 'stand out' as physically or emotionally different. There are numerous examples of how the quest for normality has resulted, historically, in educational, social or even medical interventions which are designed to reduce the outward signs of difference – to make a person appear 'normal'. Thus, there are examples of children with Down's syndrome having plastic surgery or of blind people who are taught to use certain facial expressions in order to give the impression that they are engaging with others in 'normal' ways.

Discussion point/question: Is the notion of 'normality' sustainable at a time when there is an accent on being 'different' and on 'individuality' in learning?

Further reading

Morris, J. (1993) *Independent Lives: Community Care and Disabled People.* Basingstoke: Macmillan.

See also: SEN in history; models of SEN

SCHOOL EFFECTIVENESS

Considerations of school effectiveness and SEN have provided a focal point for a great deal of discussion in recent years. This can be traced back to the period immediately following the **Education Act 1988** in which schools were given greater freedom to select their intake of pupils, whilst, on the other hand, parents were given a greater freedom of choice. One manifestation of this new way of operating was the advent of 'league tables' of schools, in which individual schools were ranked according to their academic performance. The latter placed a heavy emphasis on public examination results and the SATs (standardised assessment tests) scores. Other, non-academic factors, such as exclusions, were also featured. The higher up the performance table a school appeared, the more 'effective' it was deemed to be.

Given this greater flexibility, the position of the pupil with SEN became, for some schools, problematic. Such pupils would mainly not achieve a high academic level and in consequence would negatively impact on the school's status as an effective school. The less well a school did, the less popular it became with prospective parents, whilst increasing the level of competition for entry into those schools higher up the league table.

This resulted in the notion of a 'sink school'. These were schools in, often, disadvantaged locations, with a higher than average level of pupils who underachieved and a higher than average proportion of pupils with SEN. They were also characterised by frequent changes in teaching staff and difficulties in recruiting well-qualified staff in key curriculum areas. Perversely, such schools were frequently referred to by inspectors from the Office for Standards in Education, Children's Services and Skills (Ofsted) as 'failing schools', irrespective of the level of difficulties they faced or the relative progress that they sometimes made with pupils who present them with significant challenges.

In 1999, Norwich and Lunt proposed the key question in relation to SEN: can effective schools be **inclusive** schools? In considering this question a number of issues need to be taken into account. First, whilst school leaders are recognised as subscribing to the principle of inclusion, their commitment appears less apparent in the light of the practical impact on their school's performance or its reputation. Second, there has been some consideration of the notion of 'value-added' measures of effectiveness. This takes account of the starting points of the pupils in an effort to measure the impact that the school has had on pupil progress. However, the concept of 'value added' appears to carry less weight with parents, whose principal determinants of 'effectiveness' are a school's capacity to deliver consistently high levels of success in public examinations.

Discussion point/question: Is it compatible with high achievement and overall 'effectiveness' that a mainstream school follows a policy of 'full inclusion'?

Further reading

Farrell, P., Dyson, A., Polat, F., Hutcheson, G. and Gallannaugh, F. (2007) 'The relationship between inclusion and academic achievement in English mainstream schools', *School Effectiveness and School Improvement*, 18(3), 335–52.

See also: Education 'Reform' Act; Inclusive Schooling; inclusion and individual rights

SEN AND GLOBALISATION

A number of notable challenges for SEN in the twenty-first century have been identified as a result of the rapid increase in globalisation (Daniels and Garner, 1999). Globalisation, in practical rather than ideological terms, is best summarised by a movement towards integration of economies, with free movement of people, resources, capital and technology, resulting in an inevitable blurring of national boundaries, as well as increased competition for these various human goods and services. Its effect on education systems worldwide has been profound, but perhaps nowhere as marked as in the field of SEN.

First, over the last few years, increased globalisation has meant that there has been an unprecedented growth in the so-called 'knowledge society'. This places significant demands on education systems to provide young people for the labour market who are trained in specific areas of human activity, thus guaranteeing their usefulness to nation-states in an increasingly competitive world economic market. The pre-eminence of managerial and technological problem-solving activity, alongside the diminution of intensive manual labour in many countries, and its emergence in an increasing number of developing countries, has led to further marginalisation of those who do not possess the necessary skills or aptitudes to compete. It is argued that those children and young people who have SEN are significantly disadvantaged in such a situation.

Second, the globalisation of individual differences, as manifest by disability or SEN, has prompted further marginalisation of these groups and the commodification of 'need'. Giroux (2000) observed that the rise of the market has been accompanied by 'insidious consumer-based appropriations of freedom and choice'. In England, for example, 'choice' in education is readily accessible only to those who have the benefit of the social and cultural capital by which preferences are determined. Parents or carers of children experiencing

SEN regularly encounter difficulty in enrolling their child(ren) in a school of their choice, as the reality of open competition between schools to attract those pupils who will meet standardised attainment targets more easily or quickly. Those who present 'learning difficulties' are viewed negatively (Cooper, 1993) because their 'difference' runs contrary to the process of commodification, with its need to standardise 'products' or 'services' in order to secure economies of scale and to deliver 'profit' through measurement in officially sanctioned school league tables.

The impact of (lack of) choice in these circumstances also results in a third, more local, manifestation of globalisation. As schools become selective about who they will or will not accept on roll, so too their catchments become enlarged as they try to ensure selection of the most academically capable pupils. Many schools, particularly secondary, no longer have a discrete local function as an educational and social gathering point. Neighbourhoods, as a result, become fractured, and social relationships start to become impaired. In such circumstances, the SEN child is more likely to become isolated as their sense of belonging and **inclusion** becomes ever more tenuous.

Similar situations occur on an international scale, and when aligned with a further characteristic of globalisation in special education – the 'privatisation of 'need' – there are signals of meltdown for marginalised communities and individuals. The privatisation of education in an increasing number of countries has turned 'education' into 'big business'. In Southwark, a borough of London, the education service was contracted out to a private company. Elsewhere, Kenway and Bullen (2001) have noted similar trends in the marketisation of Australian schooling. They point out that the quantification of 'success' in such circumstances is narrow, and serves the needs of the corporation and the country, rather than those of individual children and young people. Those with SEN are expensive to cater for, difficult to assess in terms of performance, and are seen to reflect negatively on the reputation of individual schools or their sponsoring commercial partners.

The rapid corporatisation of education has also failed to attend to the differential learning needs of children and young people with SEN. The rise of managerialism in many education systems is a particular feature of this. Those in authority are encouraged and trained as 'managers', and in functioning as such are charged with 'delivering' the 'right' outcomes. These are invariably sets of targets which are unreachable (or contested) by many with SEN. Partly as a result of this, SEN and inclusion are now dominated by procedures and processes which are determined from the centre (a case in point being the **Code of Practice (2001)** which some argue emphasises regulation via a restricted set of routines, rather than encouraging teachers to respond creatively to individual learners). The widespread adoption of managerial hierarchies, each with gate-keeping functions, ensures that children are sifted into groups according to very narrow versions of cognitive ability, creativity or physical capacity. Moreover, these mechanisms are used to measure the performance of children (and schools), with the net result that those who underperform are further isolated.

One further impact of globalisation, linked closely to the notion of financial 'effectiveness', is what has been termed the 'balkanisation' of SEN. Here the tendency is for **categories of SEN** to be reinforced to ensure access to resources and support. Pressure groups and organisations, as well as professional stakeholders, seek to secure the educational and social rights of a distinct grouping of children whose needs fall into a predetermined category, be this 'dyslexic', 'autistic', or any of the categorisations currently in use. The net effect is frequently negative, with one SEN interest group campaigning for resources often at the expense of others: a microcosm, in fact, of economic globalisation.

Discussion point/question: To what extent should SEN provision be subject to the same rules of the 'marketplace' as other aspects of contemporary life? Should disability 'have a price'?

Further reading

Dos Santos, M. (2001) 'Special education, inclusion and globalisation: A few considerations inspired in the Brazilian case', *Disability and Society*, 16(2), 311–25.

See also: controversial issues; categories of SEN

SEN IN HISTORY

As with other educational ideas and movements, there are a number of defining events in the history of SEN. An acknowledgement of these allows both scholars and practitioners to understand the dramatic changes that have taken place in both policy and practice in such a relatively short period of time. It also illustrates something of the way in which education policy is, necessarily, linked to the dominant belief systems of the day.

Educational provision for children with SEN can be traced back to the eighteenth century, although it is likely that some even earlier attempts have remained unrecorded. One early pioneer was Valentin Haüy, who opened a school in Paris for the blind in 1784. This was closely followed by those of Louis Braille, whose writing system for the blind remains in common use. Around this time, too, attempts were directed at educating deaf children with the development of a standardised sign language; this historical innovation is again still in widespread use. Attention was also directed towards the education of so-called 'mentally retarded' children in the early part of the nineteenth century. Itard (1775–1838) is a key figure here. His efforts to train a feral child known as the 'Wild Boy of Aveyron' were well documented and influential. Others working with children with SEN soon followed, and major theorists such as Séguin (1812–80) and Montessori (1870–1952) began to emerge, their focus being frequently directed toward children who experienced SEN.

It is important to recognise that during the nineteenth century many children were considered to be ineducable. Formal education was not seen as appropriate for such 'defectives', and in large part they were consigned to special settings, asylums or mental institutions.

Children with motor disabilities, once considered subjects for special education, are usually integrated into the standard classroom, often by means of wheelchairs and modified desks. Children with learning disabilities and speech problems usually require specialised techniques, often on an individual basis. For children with behavioural and emotional difficulties, special therapeutic and clinical services may be provided.

Children with special needs have always been part of society, although it is only from the 1970s that the notion of SEN has been widely utilised. In the past, some 'special' education was provided to individual children on a one-to-one basis, such as Itard's previously mentioned work. As formal education became established, welfare or religious groups for the care of children with special needs often became involved in their education. Government provision of special education services generally followed the work of voluntary groups.

Progress in special education thinking saw a major reversal as the eugenics movement took hold in the early part of the twentieth century. According to eugenics theory, it was irresponsible to care for and educate people with special needs as it would 'weaken society'. Eventually, scientific approaches to studying disability, such as behavioural approaches to learning, led to a new understanding of special education and the increasingly widespread acceptance that all children could learn (as demonstrated, for example, in the work of educationists such as Skinner, Pavlov and Jerome Bruner), irrespective of what diagnosis they were given. Whilst there will always be a regrettable tendency for a small minority to hold deficit views regarding the role in society of disabled people – and famously here one brings to mind the regrettable public musings of a well-known coach of the England football team – the post-Warnock view is more optimistic. Children and adults with SEN are viewed as making a positive and welcome contribution to communities and society at large.

Discussion point/question: Do you think that social attitudes to disability have changed over the years? What evidence would you use to justify the assertion you make?

Further reading

Wearmouth, J. (2001) 'The Warnock Report: The historical background', in J. Wearmouth (ed.) *Special Educational Provision in the Context of Inclusion*. London: David Fulton, 5–35.

See also: early SEN legislation; historical 'language' of SEN; models of SEN

SOCIAL CLASS

The use of social class to both explain the prevalence of, and responses to, SEN has a long history. Moreover, it is an explanatory theme which still carries a level of currency and as such remains an important topic for consideration in any discussion regarding SEN. Having said that, any discussion which links social class and SEN is likely to be controversial in that it can carry inferences of a deficit view of certain communities. Indeed, the very use of terms such as 'working class' or 'lower class' appear to be as outmoded as they are contentious. Moreover, whilst some would regard social-class issues as a theme which has diminished in importance because of wider access to economic and cultural capital, others maintain that the impact of a widening divide between the 'haves and have-nots' has made a continued scrutiny of these issues vital to our understanding of SEN.

Research in education contains many examples of a strong association between social class and SEN. The consensus view is that, for a wide variety of reasons, the incidence of SEN is likely to increase as one moves lower down a social-class rating scale. Some research makes inferences only regarding this linkage (for example, the Bullock Report of 1975), whilst other studies purport to connect social class and SEN more explicitly.

Before considering the potential dangers of making assumptions about social class and SEN, it is worth considering the range of explanations that have been provided for their association. The high level of literacy difficulties amongst pupils from lower-class groups in England has often been attributed to the lack of reading materials at home, an absence of verbal stimulation, the failures of parents to model good reading habits, and for children from such families to have a restricted range of linguistic expression.

Alternatively, there is considerable evidence of links between physical and sensory impairments in children and the pregnancy experience of the mother. Some working-class mothers are less able to make use of antenatal care facilities, for instance, because of the distance they would need to travel. This financial inability to pay for resources to ensure that stress in pregnancy is minimised (for example, working-class mothers are less likely to have access to cars or taxis, relying on public transport to reach antenatal care facilities), implies both potential physical impacts of both fetus and newly born child, as well as the emotional duress of the mother.

A further view is that discussion of social-class issues and SEN should not be focused on 'lower-class' groups, given that, with changing patterns in families (for example, the increased levels of divorce and the traumas that children can experience as a result), many SEN can be identified across the whole school population, irrespective of **disadvantage** or cultural capital (for example, substance or alcohol abuse leading to school-underachievement or mental-health issues).

As stated, however, the question of linking social-class considerations with SEN is fraught with difficulties, and these have been the subject of ongoing discussion in education. The association has traditionally carried inferences that pupils with SEN from working-class families were the product of feckless parenting and of domestic breakdown or struggle. The debate surrounding this issue continues at the present time, and is highly charged from political, educational and moral standpoints. Arguably it might be more advantageous to remove the 'class' from the term, so that the social conditions in which people live are seen more properly as potential causes of SEN.

This avoids the controversial and unsustainable correlation between social status and learning difficulty.

Discussion point/question: Does the ethos and character of the schools located in an area you are familiar with tell you anything about their likely position in published 'league tables' of educational performance?

Further reading

Slee, R. (1996) 'Disability, social class and poverty: School structures and policing identities', in C. Christensen and F. Rizvi (eds) *Disability and the Dilemmas of Education and Justice*. Buckingham: Open University Press, 96–118.

See also: disadvantage; extended schools

DEFINITIONS AND
TERMINOLOGY

CATEGORIES OF SEN

When children and young people are the subject of professional assessment, on account of concerns being expressed that their learning or social behaviour appears not to be consistent with that of the majority of others at a similar age, the end result is the attribution of a category or term which summarises the pupils' capabilities and aptitudes. Such categories can be either non-formal (school based) or officially attributed. In the case of the former, pupils are defined as having a stated SEN when they are assessed as part of **School Action** or **School Action Plus**, the two stage process adopted by the **Code of Practice (2001)**. This non-formal process is an important element of intervention in that it is a necessary step towards a pupil with significant SEN receiving a legally binding '**statement of special educational needs**'. And even at the school level of assessment, the **special educational needs coordinator** (SENCO) and other specialist teachers are aware of distinctions between the current categories of SEN.

The language used historically in categorisation appears now to be heavily deficit laden and even pejorative. In 1889, for instance, the Egerton Commission identified three categories of mentally handicapped children: 'idiots', 'imbeciles' and the 'feeble minded'. Such expressions were entirely consistent with the thinking of the day. Later, the Mental Deficiency Acts of 1913 and 1914, based on the newly discovered intelligence tests, are further official testimony of the understanding of the time – that learning difficulties were caused wholly by deficiencies in the child.

Current practice, enshrined in the 2001 Code, refers to just four categories or groupings of SEN. These relate to (i) **communication and interaction**, (ii) **cognition and learning**, (iii) **behaviour, emotional and social** development and (iv) **sensory and/or physical** needs. The Code also makes recommendations for pupils with medical conditions. These are general terms within which are subsumed pupils who have a diverse range of individual needs and conditions. And it is equally important to recognise that there can be overlap between the categories, so that a pupil who has a communication difficulty might, because of personal frustration at not being able to relate effectively to others, display unwanted problem behaviour too.

The following entries provide an illustration of the range and complexity of learning difficulties covered in each of the current groupings of SEN. It is important to remember, though, that each of

41

the four broad categorisations given comprises such a diverse array of syndromes, SEN and disabilities that space does not allow every single one to be mentioned in this book. Those included are for illustration only, and do not indicate their greater importance or significance amongst a far greater number of individual needs.

Discussion point/question: Is the move from more explicit 'categories', as introduced, for example, in the 1944 Education Act, to more general terms like 'learning difficulties' or SEN particularly helpful to practitioners in schools?

Further reading

Fulcher, G. (1990) *Disabling Policies? A Comparative Approach to Education Policy and Disability*. London: Falmer Press.

(a) communication and interaction

(i) autism

This special educational need was identified as late as the 1940s. It is characterised by impairments to all forms of communication and a difficulty in judging the appropriateness of actions in social settings resulting in an inability to develop normal social relationships. It is also apparent that autistic children demonstrate rigidity and inflexibility in the way they perceive things, resulting in inflexible behaviour. The latter can be manifest by bizarre mannerisms and habits, and obsessional behaviour. Sometimes there are significant physical characteristics too: approximately a third of autistic children are inclined to suffer from epileptic fits, for example.

Autism is diagnosed nearly always within the first 30 months of a child's life. It is a condition which, like many other SEN, affects more boys than girls: three times more boys than girls experience autism. Approximately five children per 1000 have autism in its classic form, whilst three or four times as many children can have a range of autistic-like symptoms. This has resulted in the introduction of the widely accepted general term 'autistic spectrum disorder' (ASD).

Early explanations of autism focused on psychological causation. Kanner, who first identified the condition, thought that it was the product of a lack of warmth and demonstrativeness on the part of parents. More recently it has been accepted that autism, like other SEN, is mainly multifactorial in cause, and that such things as neurological impairment, biochemical abnormality and childhood illness are all implicated in some way. Notoriously, the cause of autism has recently come under the spotlight, with the claims of one researcher that autism is linked to the MMR (measles, mumps and rubella) vaccination in childhood. Such claims have largely been shown to be erroneous.

About three quarters of autistic pupils experience either severe or moderate learning difficulties. It is important to bear this in mind, because the media portrayal of autistic people is inclined to emphasise the relatively small number of cases where an autistic person has a particular and very exceptional talent: such an instance was famously portrayed in the film *Rain Man*. Although an increasing number of autistic pupils attend **mainstream settings**, many attend **special schools**. The latter are viewed as one way of ensuring that a more structured educational environment with systematic procedures and teaching is available. These conditions are viewed as vital in addressing the needs of these children.

Discussion point/question: Do you think that media portrayals of autistic people tend to glamorise them, when in fact the reality is that they encounter great difficulties, prejudice and isolation?

Further reading

Alderson, P. and Goodey, C. (1999) 'Autism in special and inclusive schools: There has to be a point to their being there', *Disability & Society*, 14(2), 249–61.

(ii) speech and language disorder

Children who are unable to use language (either verbal or non-verbal) effectively can experience cognitive or emotional difficulties as well as problems in interaction socially. Some theorists regard 'speech' impairments as something relating to the physical actions of speaking, and thus relate to such things as stuttering, lisping and pronunciation difficulties. Language difficulties, on the other hand, would be viewed by the same theorists as relating to the problem that a child might experience because of a lack of vocabulary, for instance. Both 'speech' and 'language' interrelate however, and this has resulted in their inclusion in an overarching term, 'speech and language disorder'.

In broad terms, speech and language disorder is currently viewed as relating to two areas: receptive and expressive disorders. The former relate to such vital areas as listening or reading, whilst expressive language places emphasis on speaking and writing. All these aspects of communication are subsumed within the government's **National Literacy Strategy**, introduced in 2001. This was designed to improve standards of literacy in the general school population, although it does have important implications for children whose SEN are related to speech and language.

The causes for speech and language disorder include both biological and environmental factors. The former may relate, for example, to hearing impairments or neurological factors which might cause coordination difficulties resulting in poor handwriting skills. Environmental factors, on the other hand, refer to such things as early experiences of an environment in which language use is relatively restricted, or in cases where a child is not encouraged to experiment in language use or does not have opportunities to model language.

It is difficult to provide any precise figures regarding the incidence of pupils who have speech and language disorder. One problematic issue relates to the close overlap between this category of SEN and many others. For example, dyslexia might be referred to as a speech and language disorder (or, at least, impairments of speech and language might be one of the characteristics of dyslexia). A similar proposition could be made regarding hearing impairment or emotional and behavioural difficulty (where difficulties in communication can result in frustration, anger and an unwanted acting-out behaviour). The government's Annual Statistical Release of 2007 indicates that about 14 per cent of the total SEN population in schools in England experience speech and language disorder.

Responses to these difficulties are varied. At a generic level, the National Literacy Strategy identifies a range of teaching interventions, and most primary schools have a 'literacy coordinator', who will work with the **special educational needs coordinator** to address a pupil's difficulties in speech and language. A range of specialised services are also available, including **speech therapists**, audiologists and **educational psychologists**. In addition, most local authorities have dedicated speech and language services which provide resources and advice to schools in this area of SEN.

Discussion point/question: Why is it important for us to view the effective development of speech and language as one of the most crucial life skills for children with SEN?

Further reading

Conti-Ramsden, G. and Botting, N. (2004) 'Social difficulties and victimisation in children with SLI at 11 years of age', *Journal of Speech, Language and Hearing Research,* 47(1), 145–72.

(iii) selective mutism

This condition refers to cases where a child who is able to speak refuses to do so. It is frequently the case that such mutism is context specific, in that the child may choose to talk normally at home or in some other social settings but not in school. It is sometimes referred to as elective mutism, although this expression can misleadingly infer that a child has some level of choice in the matter. There appears to be no physical or cognitive reason for its occurrence. It is a very low-level occurrence compared to other SEN.

The principal explanations for selective mutism are behavioural and psychological. In the case of behavioural factors, some theorists and professionals argue that the child has learned that his or her silence brings with it some kind of reward. Over time this self-perception is reinforced; in some cases the child will view attention from a significant adult (in this case, for instance, an **educational psychologist** or therapist) as a reward, thereby reinforcing their selective mutism. Psychological explanations, on the other hand, relate to a traumatic life event or series of events, resulting in feelings of withdrawal or hostility. Many children who experience selective mutism have a predisposition to anxiety.

As with other SEN outlined in these sections, there will be some overlap with other difficulties. Selective mutism, therefore, might be one manifestation of an emotional difficulty or mental-health problem. It is estimated that about 20 per cent of pupils who are selectively mute also have attendant speech and language disorder. A further complicating factor is that in young children selective mutism can sometimes be confused with autistic spectrum disorders.

Discussion point/question: How is it possible for a teacher to detect whether a pupil is selectively mute, as opposed to having a particular speech and language disorder?

Further reading

Omdal, H. (2008) 'Including children with selective mutism in mainstream schools and kindergartens: Problems and possibilities', *International Journal of Inclusive Education,* 12(3), 301–15.

(b) cognition and learning

(i) dyslexia

In very general terms, a pupil whose SEN is referred to as 'dyslexia' will have significant difficulties in reading, writing and spelling. Importantly, these difficulties will not be those which are consistent with the pupil's general intellectual ability. This discrepancy may also result in other behaviours, notably withdrawn or acting-out behaviour and 'clumsiness', whilst links between dyslexia and attention deficit disorder have also been made. As a term, it is one of the most contested and debated topics in the whole of SEN.

It is important to note that a more general term, specific learning difficulties (SpLD), has been applied to dyslexia. But the term SpLD is also used to describe a learning difficulty affecting an ability with numbers (dyscalculia).

A wide range of explanations for dyslexia have been proposed. Originally the term was used in neurology to describe reading difficulties amongst adults which were caused by brain damage. The word itself comes from the Greek, meaning 'a difficulty with words'. This early focus on neurology provides clues to one of the more widely popularised explanations for dyslexia – that of neurological differences. Dyslexic children appear to have a larger right hemisphere in their brains than those of other pupils. Some theorists argue that right-brain dependence is one explanation for why dyslexic pupils have aptitudes in such areas controlled by the right side of the brain, such as artistic skills, musical talent, problem solving and 'people skills', all of which are associated with right-brain dominance.

There is also a commonly held view that dyslexia is inherited. Indeed, researchers have identified a dominant gene which may explain this. But other contrasting explanations show the lack of general agreement on what causes dyslexia. Central to this is the contested nature of the term itself. Thus, some very well-qualified academics, teachers and other professionals have maintained that dyslexia is something of a myth in that it is a 'middle-class' term for underachievement in reading. This kind of thinking is fuelled by those who have claimed that the teaching interventions used to address dyslexia are no different to those used for 'underachieving readers'.

Estimates regarding the incidence of dyslexia vary, although currently it is maintained that about 12 per cent of the total SEN population is identified as dyslexic. But such estimates need to be handled with caution, given that there is much debate regarding the very nature of the SEN.

Discussion point/question: Is dyslexia, as is claimed by some critics, a 'middle-class special educational need'?

Further reading

Peer, L. and Reid, G. (2003) *Introduction to Dyslexia*. London: David Fulton.

(ii) (hand)writing difficulties

Handwriting is traditionally viewed as one of the three 'Rs' (reading, 'riting and 'rithmetic). Whilst it has received considerable attention historically, some have argued that the increased use of computers in schools has somewhat marginalised handwriting as a skill. None the less, it remains part of the **National Literacy Strategy**. Many children, across a range of SEN, have difficulty in writing. Broadly speaking, these difficulties can be divided into those which have physiological origins and those which relate to a pupil's psychological and emotional functioning.

In the case of physiological factors, children who have coordination difficulties, including poor motor control, find handwriting difficult. Lack of consistent and developed control of fingers and hands makes writing a very difficult task. It has been argued that the early stages of children's education (the 'Foundation Stage') do not place sufficient emphasis on the development of manual dexterity so that some children arrive in primary school unable to cope with the fine movement required for proficient handwriting.

It is also the case that handwriting development is incremental, and that it is linked to maturation and clumsiness, both of which relate to a child's developmental stage. It has also been noted that children who are left-handed experience greater difficulties with handwriting – this is because the left hand has to push the pen across the page (rather than pull it as is the case with right-handed writers).

Children with neuromuscular problems, like cerebral palsy, often have extreme difficulty in this area of the literacy curriculum and many use communication aids to support their learning. Pupils who have had head injuries or who experience certain medical problems may also have difficulties in writing.

Handwriting can be negatively affected by psychological and emotional factors. As an activity, handwriting incorporates both cognitive and physical skills. It is also an activity which is more time consuming than (for example) either speaking or listening. In cases where a pupil has difficulty in concentrating because of emotional trauma, or a feeling of boredom or alienation from the curriculum, poor handwriting is one of the first indicators of distraction and lack of involvement.

There are few reliable estimates concerning the prevalence of handwriting difficulties.

Discussion point/question: Do boys always have poorer handwriting than girls? If so, what are the possible explanations?

Further reading

Rosenblum S., Weiss P. and Parush S. (2003) 'Product and process evaluation of handwriting difficulties', *Educational Psychology Review*, 15(1), 41–81.

(iii) dyscalculia

Dyscalculia concerns the difficulty children experience in understanding mathematics. Research suggests that dyscalculia occurs, in part, as a result of developmental dysfunction. Although scientists have still much to discover about dyscalculia, it is regarded, in part, as a genetically linked, neurologically based learning disability, affecting the child's capacity to make sense of, remember and meaningfully manage numbers and number facts (for example, multiplication tables, or 'rules' of addition or subtraction). The word dyscalculia originates from the Greek and, very approximately, means 'counting inefficiently or badly'. As such, it is viewed as a somewhat less well-known learning difficulty but potentially related to dyslexia and dyspraxia. As with the latter two SEN, dyscalculia can occur in children irrespective of their ability (for example, as measured by their intelligence quota (IQ)). Frequently the difficulties these children encounter will extend into adult life, and will be manifest in such things as difficulties with time, measurement and spatial reasoning. It is estimated that 3–5 per cent of the whole population experiences difficulties presented by dyscalculia. **Educational psychologists** view it as being the pupil's incapacity to deal with numbers as abstract concepts.

As with many other SEN, dyscalculia can be detected at an early stage and subsequent interventions can significantly minimise the difficulties experienced by young people. A key to remediation is changing the way mathematics is taught to children.

Discussion point/question: Is dyscalculia simply an official term for children who are not very good at maths?

Further reading

Bird, R. (2007) *The Dyscalculia Toolkit – Supporting Learning Difficulties in Maths*. London: Sage.

(c) behaviour, emotional and social

(i) eating disorders

Children whose SEN relate to the behavioural, emotional and social impacts of their eating patterns are described as having eating disorders. This group of SEN are represented by a complex diversity of disorders which have mainly psychological and social underpinnings.

Some children, for a variety of psychological or psychosocial reasons, deliberately limit the amount of food they eat. As a result they rapidly lose weight, which can result in serious physiological complications. Anorexia nervosa can lead to some children losing as much as 50 per cent of their total body weight. This disorder, which is underpinned by a morbid and irrational fear of becoming obese, is prevalent mainly amongst adolescent girls: those aged between 12 and 18 years are most significantly at risk, although there are some indications that anorexia is becoming an issue amongst boys. Incidence rates for this disorder are estimated to be 1 in 200.

Explanations of anorexia nervosa mainly focus on the notion that some children are unable to comfortably leave a 'childhood state', which manifests into the child wanting a small body mass. A further psychological factor is that the anorexic has learned to link slimness with qualities which are recognised (through the media and role models amongst peer groups) with social acceptance, attractiveness and desirability. Important amongst the psychosocial factors is the (feminist) view that anorexia is connected with the traditional function of women in society: society is dominated by men, who may have a restricted and stereotypical view of the appearance and demeanour of women.

The impact of anorexia can be lifelong. Regrettably there is a high level of mortality resulting from the condition, with some estimates being as high as 20 per cent of the anorexic population.

Malnutrition, on the other hand, has been associated with under-performance in school. It can also result in irritability, failure to concentrate and potential involvement in unwanted, challenging behaviours. One way in which this has been tackled in recent years has been the establishment of so-called 'breakfast clubs', which provide meals for pupils who arrive in school without breakfast. The rationale for this approach is based on the theory of Maslow, who argued that unless certain basic physiological needs were met, children would not thrive. Food, along with shelter and clothing, comprised the core needs of all humans.

A further eating disorder, which can be a causal factor for SEN, is obesity.

Discussion point/question: Are childhood eating disorders a contemporary problem? At what stage do they become a 'special educational need'?

Further reading

Honey, H., Boughtwood, D., Clarke, S., Halse, C., Kohn, M. and Madden, S. (2008) 'Support for parents of children with anorexia: What parents want', *Eating Disorders*, 16(1), 40–51.

(ii) attention deficit (hyperactivity) disorder

Attention deficit (hyperactivity) disorder (ADHD) is a neuro-behavioural disorder. It is obvious in early childhood, although it is now increasingly diagnosed amongst the adult population. Of the children who are diagnosed as having ADHD, around two thirds will continue to retain the difficulty into their adult lives. Current estimates suggest that ADHD affects around 3–5 per cent of the population.

ADHD is characterised by an ongoing inability to concentrate or be 'attentive' in given situations, alongside a frequent higher than usual level of acting-out behaviour, presented as impulsivity, forgetfulness and a susceptibility to distraction. Children who experience ADHD are more inclined to have difficulties in organising their school work, have difficulties with punctuality and find forward planning to be problematic. These behaviours are not isolated events: ADHD is a condition in which the child demonstrates a pronounced pattern of these characteristics. It is also associated with other serious SEN, such as oppositional defiance disorder and conduct disorders, indicators of both being extreme aggression, temper tantrums and antisocial behaviour (for example, stealing). In some cases ADHD can lead to anxiety disorders or other mental-health issues.

It is now widely accepted that ADHD is mainly **genetic** in causation, although there are certain environmental factors (diet, prenatal alcohol consumption by mother, domestic trauma, lead pollution) which can play an important role. Moreover, the scientific study of ADHD is still in its relative infancy, and researchers have been understandably reserved in making definitive claims for its causation. In fact, it is probably wise to regard genetic and environmental factors as linked in a complex, multifactorial model of causation, especially given that researchers have as yet been unable to categorically identify a gene which has a major correlation with the incidence of ADHD.

Intervention strategies for ADHD have been the subject of considerable controversy in recent years. The growth of medical intervention has been pronounced and has some extremely vociferous advocates – not least many parents, who view medication as providing not only a controlled regime for the child in which learning can at least begin to take place, but also as an important contribution to their own capacity to deal with their child's ADHD. Critics have termed the use of pharmaceuticals to 'control' the behaviour of children as a 'chemical cosh'. Behavioural approaches can be successful, building on the understanding that some ADHD behaviours have been learned and that they can therefore be unlearned.

The prognosis for children with ADHD is mixed, although frequent negative outcomes are reported. Thus children will show significant levels of academic underachievement in school, and as such will require inputs from specialist (SEN) teachers and other professionals. They will also be over-represented amongst those who experience **exclusion** on account of their unacceptable behaviour. A diagnosis of ADHD in reality means the likelihood of impairments in life functioning, with only small percentages of the ADHD population going on to study beyond compulsory schooling and many becoming involved in delinquency and subsequent criminality.

Discussion point/question: Is ADHD simply a new expression coined to enable children who present certain challenging behaviours to be categorised in order that they receive support and resources?

Further reading

Cooper, P. and O'Regan, F. (2001) *Educating Children with ADHD*. London: Routledge.

(iii) emotional and behavioural difficulties

Pupils with emotional and behavioural difficulties (EBD) present a diverse range of challenges to teachers. Pupils designated as 'EBD' can exhibit behaviours ranging on a continuum from relatively minor, although frequent, infringements of school rules through to severe forms of aggressive, acting-out behaviour. The behaviour continuum is regarded to range from the 'normal but unacceptable' through to those behaviours which are associated with significant emotional dysfunction and mental illness. In terms of specific behaviour, the continuum can be illustrated by acts of continued disobedience and refusal to comply with agreed school rules at one end, through to those actions which are physically aggressive and aimed at damaging others.

Because the spectrum of EBD is so wide and ranges from straight-forward naughtiness through to quite complex psychiatric disorders, and from behaviours that are at best irritating and annoying to those which are extremely challenging, there has always been a struggle for an adequate definition of the term. The SEN **Code of Practice** attempts to provide a lengthy definition and includes terms such as 'withdrawn', 'isolated', 'disruptive', 'disturbing', 'hyperactive', 'lacking concentration' and presenting 'challenging behaviour'. Each of these terms, though, is only marginally helpful because they are generic expressions and do nothing to recognise that behaviour needs to be seen and described in context and to be recorded in explicit, understandable terms. Critics argue that expressions such as 'isolated' or 'disruptive' are too general and can be interpreted differently by various professionals or others. One positive aspect of the SEN Code of Practice's attempt at definition was that it sought to connect EBD with the social difficulties that such children invariably encountered. The expression 'behavioural, emotional and social difficulties' was thus established and continues to have currency.

The latter is important because many pupils who present behaviour difficulties in school also have parallel difficulties within their families and communities. They are frequently involved with the social services part of **children's services** and are also commonly associated with juvenile justice systems and the police. Many also will have mental-health issues and be already known to the local **child and adolescent mental health service**.

In just the same way that the term 'EBD' covers a range of pupil characteristics, so too is there a spectrum of causal factors associated with this SEN. Not all children with EBD have difficulties associated with their family background or social environment. EBD are also associated with genetic or biological conditions, as in the case of Tourette syndrome, ADHD and Asperger's syndrome, the symptoms and effects of which may lead to distress, frustration and, subsequently, to the development of EBD. Some EBD have also been associated with exceptionally high levels of ability. Moreover, there has been a rapid growth in understanding that schools and individual teachers have a major role to play – both as causal factors of inappropriate behaviour and as insulating agents against such actions in the first place. But, as with many other SEN, there now appears to be a firm consensus that EBD are the product of a holistic or 'ecosystemic' set of factors, all of which have significant interdependence.

Provision for EBD pupils is mainly in **mainstream schools**, although there are large numbers of pupils currently educated in **special schools** (both 'day' and residential) and in **pupil referral units** and study centres. Others benefit from home tuition. Major policy initiatives have been undertaken in recent years by the government to address the needs of these pupils, as well as in respect of generic 'behaviour management' itself.

Discussion point/question: Why should some schools, rather than others, have a greater number of pupils who exhibit EBD?

Further reading

Clough, P., Garner, P., Pardeck, T. and Yuen, F. (2005) *The Handbook of Emotional and Behavioural Difficulties*. London: Sage.

(d) sensory and/or physical

(i) brain damage/injury

Children who are born brain damaged, or who suffer serious head injuries resulting in brain damage, require specialist teaching in order to enable them to maximise their learning potential. The extent to which the brain is impaired, together with the location of the injury and the age at which it occurred will have implications for any educational intervention. Brain damage or 'acquired brain injury' is best described as the destruction or the degeneration over time of a person's brain cells. This can be the result of illness, complications (oxygen shortage) at birth or poisoning (as in the case of fetal alcohol syndrome). The term is generic, and incorporates a number of SENs, including cerebral palsy and epilepsy.

Meeting the needs of children with brain injury, in whatever form this occurs, will naturally involve various professionals working as an interdisciplinary team: medical doctors, psychologists, rehabilitation specialists (for example, **occupational therapists**), teachers and others. Children who are brain damaged are educated in both **mainstream** and **special schools**, although the most serious cases are provided for in specialist units within these.

Discussion point/question: There are obviously various levels of brain injury in children. Investigate the concept of 'minimal brain dysfunction': what does it tell you?

Further reading

Arroyos-Jurado E., Paulsen J., Merrell K., Lindgren S. and Max J. (2000) 'Traumatic brain injury in school-age children: Academic and social outcome', *Journal of School Psychology*, 38(6), 571–87.

(ii) visual impairment

Visual impairment refers to the loss of vision, usually resulting from disease or from a congenital condition. The term refers to a range of conditions, all of which have an impact on a child's learning. There are approximately 20,000 blind and partially sighted children and young people in England. Of these around 50 per cent have no other disabilities, whilst approximately 30 per cent have additional complex needs including severe learning difficulties (SLD) or profound and multiple learning difficulties (PMLD), and around 18 per cent have additional disabilities other than SLD or PMLD.

As stated, visual impairment ranges from (relatively) minor disabilities like short-sightedness, extending through to such conditions as colour blindness, more significant loss of sight (partially blind) through to blindness.

Visual impairment can be caused by a range of factors, including malformation of the cornea, lens or globe of the eye and the effects of rubella at birth. Some visual impairments are hereditary, as in the case of retinitis pigmentosa, which causes a degeneration of the retina, and muscular problems that result in involuntary eye movement.

In educational terms, a child is regarded as 'blind' if he or she requires, predominantly, one or more non-sighted methods of learning, including, for example, Braille. Local authorities have designated advisers, many of whom work exclusively with pupils who have visual impairments. They, and teachers and specialist **teaching assistants**, will interact closely with health services in meeting the needs of children with visual impairments. In the indicative case of one local authority (Barnet in Greater London), this will include:

- Direct support to visually impaired pupils in mainstream education and to preschool children and their parents in the home environment;
- Assessments and reports on pupils' visual functioning and the resulting implications for teaching and learning;
- Advice and support to special schools with visually impaired pupils;
- In-service training in support of pupil placement;
- Individual teaching of specific skills such as the use of access technology and Braille;
- Liaising closely with parents and developing home/school links – this includes arranging parent get-togethers for information sharing and mutual support;
- Working closely with other professionals, such as medical personnel, social workers and voluntary organisations, to ensure total child care;
- Adaptation of curriculum materials into Braille, speech and preferential-size print;
- Contributing to individual education and access programmes;
- Advice on placement for students and their parents in colleges of further education.

As with other SEN, children who have visual impairments are educated both in mainstream and special schools. Where the former obtains, specialist support is provided, either within the school itself or in the form of peripatetic services, which move from one school to another as required and as illustrated in the case of Barnet local authority. Support will take the form of collaborative planning of appropriate interventions, and advice on the curriculum itself and on the specialist resources required for the child to learn effectively. Another major role in the context of the mainstream school is to provide advice to the whole school on how best to support blind or partially sighted pupils.

Braille, as has been noted, is perhaps the most common form of enabling blind pupils to access the printed word. It comprises a system of raised dots which are set out in different positions, each cluster representing different letters, whole words or punctuation. Normally a blind child will take about three times as long to read Braille than a sighted child takes to read the same printed piece.

Discussion point/question: To what extent can their peers in class provide support for children who have visual impairments? Is it a realistic expectation that they do so?

Further reading

Davis, P. (2003) *Including Children with Visual Impairment in Mainstream Schools: A Practical Guide*. London: David Fulton.

(iii) epilepsy

Epilepsy is a condition which usually develops before a person reaches the age of 20, and is manifested by recurrent seizures because the brain cells produce unusual electrical activity. Such seizures can be pronounced and severe, whilst others can be far more subtle, being characterised by changes in a child's behaviour and level of awareness. It is estimated that around 1 in 200/250 children has a form of epilepsy, and the vast majority of such children attend **mainstream schools**.

Epilepsy is a generic term which covers a spectrum of seizures (or 'fits'). These include:

- 'Petit mal', which most commonly affect children and takes the form of a brief loss of awareness, so that the child appears as though he or she is 'daydreaming'; some children experience rapid swallowing or eye flickers. Children may have repeated instances of this throughout a school day, and although these attacks can be disorientating, the child is able to return to a normal state of functioning quite rapidly after their occurrence.
- Clonic seizures are indicated by involuntary thrashing and jerking movements of the body, which are caused by the muscles relaxing and contracting repeatedly. As movement can be difficult to predict, the child experiencing a clonic seizure needs a space which is free from furniture etc. in order to prevent injury.
- 'Grand mal' seizures, often called 'tonic-clonic' seizures involve loss of consciousness, muscle stiffening and collapse (the tonic phase), followed by involuntary thrashing or jerking movements (the clonic phase).

Most children with epilepsy attend mainstream schools. Once identified, epilepsy can be managed by teachers taking into account the individual needs of each child. An awareness of the likely physiological effects on the child's learning by the teacher and/or **teaching assistant** is crucial to ensuring that such children's needs are met. Thus, it needs to be recognised that, as a general rule, attainment levels of children with epilepsy are somewhat lower than average. This can be a result of frequent drowsiness, caused both by 'petit mal' and by medication. Obviously, the inclination on the part of the teacher to interpret the child's drowsiness as boredom or disinterest needs to be carefully avoided.

Discussion point/question: What can teachers and schools best plan to manage the immediate impact on a child when he or she has a seizure?

Further reading

Johnson, M. and Parkinson, J. (2002) *Epilepsy: A Practical Guide*. London: David Fulton.

LEGISLATION AND POLICY

EDUCATION ACT 1944

The Education Act 1944 was an ambitious attempt to create a new structure for post-war British education. As with other acts, the substantive content of the 1944 legislation related to the education system in general (for example, the Act provided universal free schooling in three distinct types of school; grammar, secondary modern and technical, as well as raising the school leaving age to 15 years). R.A. Butler hoped that these schools would cater for the different academic levels and other aptitudes of children. Entry to these schools was based on the 11+ examination.

In respect of SEN, the 1944 Act established that the education that children receive should be based on their age, aptitude and 'ability' (which at that time was mainly demonstrated by 11+ testing). Eleven categories or groups of 'handicap' were described. These were: blind, partially sighted, deaf, partially deaf, delicate, diabetic, educationally subnormal, epileptic, maladjusted, physically handicapped and those with speech defects. It was the responsibility of the local education authority to determine who were handicapped, using their own often arbitrary diagnostic and assessment procedures. Illustrative of this process is the case of 'subnormality' – a handicap which was first mooted by Sir Cyril Burt in 1935. He calculated that children scoring 50–85 on mental tests should be considered as 'educationally subnormal'.

Once categorised, the child was allocated to a school or other setting. There was little involvement sought from parents or carers. Indicative of the thinking of the time was the general philosophy that the child should adjust to 'fit' the school rather than the school making any changes to its policies or operations to meet the learning difficulties of the child.

Discussion point/question: Does the way in which the 1944 Education Act categorised children with SEN have any practical value at the present time? Is this way of grouping children consistent with 'inclusive education'?

Further reading

Barton, L. and Tomlinson, S. (1984) *Special Education and Social Interests*. London: Croom Helm.

See also: categories of SEN; historical 'language' of SEN

EDUCATION (HANDICAPPED CHILDREN) ACT 1970

This Act was noteworthy in that it represented a forerunner of the notion of 'education for all' by requiring all local authorities to provide education for all children with severe mental handicaps. Previously such children were regarded as 'ineducable'. As such they constituted the very last group of children of school age to whom education had been denied. Previously their needs were catered for by the health service, which operated 'training centres' and special units often attached to hospitals.

The effects of the Act were to be of long standing. The legislation resulted in training centres being re-designated as special schools, which became centres for education. Any staff not already qualified as a teacher and who were to be transferred from a training centre to a newly designated school were required to undertake additional training.

Discussion point/question: Is there, or has there ever been, a case for saying that any child is so disabled that he or she cannot benefit from education?

Further reading

Armstrong, D. (2003) *Experiences of Special Education: Re-evaluating Policy and Practice through Life Stories*. London: Routledge.

See also: historical 'language' of SEN

WARNOCK REPORT (1978)

The Warnock Report was commissioned in 1974 by the Conservative government of the day. It was chaired by Baroness Warnock, and comprised an influential cross section of educationists, politicians, philosophers and administrators. Its brief was to review provision for children in school who had what are now termed to be SEN. The report, entitled the 'Warnock Committee of Enquiry into the Education of Handicapped Children and Young People' was delivered in 1978 and formed the basis of the subsequent **Education Act 1981**. The report was ground breaking for several reasons, not least because it broke with the traditional convention of referring to pupils with learning difficulties by such deficit-laden terms as 'remedial', 'backward' or 'educationally subnormal'.

This in itself is a remarkable legacy, as the report's promotion of more positive, empowering terminology – 'learning difficulty' and, especially, 'special educational needs' – subsequently became universally adopted in England. Thus, terms such as 'educationally subnormal' were replaced, as was the term 'remedial' in **mainstream schools**. In their place the term 'children with learning difficulties' was used, with the subdivisions of mild, moderate and severe. This formulation was the basis for the ongoing grouping of children with particular needs as having moderate learning difficulties, severe learning difficulties, and profound and multiple learning difficulties.

But the Warnock Report also provided much of the context for subsequent policy making in special education. It firmly rejected the view that there were two types of child – the handicapped and the non-handicapped. Instead it promoted the more positive concept of special educational needs, which incorporated both the learning needs and the strengths and aptitudes of each child in its description. This was the first time that the notion of SEN had been used in such a substantive and official way. Warnock estimated that approximately one in five children in schools would, at some stage in their school career, require specialist input on account of a learning difficulty.

The report went on to make several recommendations regarding how such pupils should be taught. The report suggested that provision for SEN should comprise: (a) distinct and specific ways in which the curriculum could be accessed (by specialist teaching, alternative resources or technology); (b) adaptations to the existing curriculum; and (c) making changes to the climate and ethos of the school in order to make it more open and accessible to those with SEN.

But the report did not restrict itself to recommendations regarding the school curriculum. It also had some ground-breaking (for its time) suggestions regarding empowering parents (who should, Warnock recommended, be crucial partners in their child's education and who should be consulted on all decisions regarding it), and teacher training and education provision for the early years as well as that for young people over the age of 16. Finally, Warnock provided a set of recommendations for teacher training, both initial and in-service. Many of the ideas presented in each of these areas formed the bedrock of future policy and planning in SEN.

But perhaps the most significant recommendation contained in the Warnock Report was that relating to the **integration** of pupils with learning difficulties within mainstream schools, with the report describing integration as the 'central contemporary issue in special education'.

Discussion point/question: Given that its impact in SEN has been widespread and significant, what do you think is the most important legacy of the Warnock Report's recommendations?

Further reading

Lewis, I. and Vulliamy, G. (1980) 'Warnock or Warlock? The sorcery of definitions: The limitations of the Report on Special Education', *Educational Review*, 32(1), 3–10.

See also: integration; statement; categories of SEN; special schools and settings

EDUCATION ACT 1981 — *Introduction of SEN*

The majority of the recommendations of the Warnock Report of 1978 were enshrined within the Education Act 1981. It came to be regarded as one of the defining pieces of legislation in the **history of SEN**, and its impact is still apparent today. It provided the statutory means by which Warnock 'thinking' could be operationalised at policy and practice levels, and did so in five key areas:

(i) Definition of SEN. The Act established a new framework within which children with learning difficulties should be considered. It replaced the old categories of handicap (which were established following the Education Act 1944 and included blind, maladjusted, delicate, educationally subnormal and physically handicapped) with the concept of 'special educational needs'. This defined a situation where a child has SEN if he or she has a learning difficulty which requires special educational provision. The Act went on to state that a learning difficulty occurrs when: (a) a child has significantly greater difficulty in learning than the majority of other children of that age; (b) a child has a disability which inhibits him or her from using educational facilities generally available in schools; and (c) is under five years of age and falls into either of the above groups.

(ii) The Act stated that, given certain conditions, special educational provision should be provided in mainstream settings.

(iii) A major element of the Act focused on **identification and assessment** of SEN. It stated that LEAs had a duty to identify all children with SEN in its administrative area, and to take steps to meet their needs. The formal, standardised process of assessment was instituted, in which a five-stage process led, in cases where the SEN was profound, severe and complex, to a formal **statement of SEN**, which set out how the child's educational needs would be met.

(iv) The Act gave more power to parents in that local authorities (LAs) were obliged to ensure that parents were consulted at every stage in the process of statementing, and in the subsequent annual reviews which were a legal requirement of the process.

Discussion point/question: It is claimed that the Education Act 1981 represents the most sweeping reform of special education in England. Is this true? Have subsequent pieces of legislation had a greater impact on our thinking and practice?

FURTHER READING

Solity, J. and Raybould, E. (1988) *The 1981 Education Act: A Positive Response*. Buckingham: Open University Press.

See also: identification and assessment; statement of SEN

EDUCATION 'REFORM' ACT 1988

The Education Act of 1988 is widely regarded as the most important recent piece of education legislation in England, Wales and Northern Ireland since the 'Butler' Education Act of 1944. Scottish education legislation is separate from that of the rest of the UK. Although the Act related to compulsory educational provision as a whole, it carried important implications for pupils with learning difficulties. Subsequently it was to have great impact upon pupils with SEN. Because of its wide-ranging implications across every sector of education, the Act was dubbed the 'Reform Act' by commentators and critics. The latter were to argue that 'reform' implies something for the common good, whereas much of what was proposed in this legislation appeared to run contrary to the interests of some of those most marginalised by existing educational provision, including, notably, those pupils with SEN.

The main provisions of the Education 'Reform' Act are as follows:

1. Grant maintained schools were introduced. Primary and secondary schools could, under this provision, remove themselves fully from their respective local education authority and would henceforth be completely funded by central government. Secondary schools also had limited selection powers at the age of 11.
2. The local management of schools was introduced. This part of the Act allowed all schools to be taken out of the direct financial control of LAs. Financial control would be handed to the head teacher and the governors of a school
3. A **National Curriculum** was introduced.
4. Key stages were introduced in schools. At each key stage, a number of educational objectives were to be achieved.
5. An element of choice was introduced, where parents could specify which school was their preferred choice.
6. League tables, publishing the examination results of schools, were introduced.

The impact of these measures on SEN was profound. For example, the increase in the powers given to schools meant that they would be in a position to invoke some form of selection of their pupil intake which would clearly impact negatively on some children (at the very least) with particular SEN. The devolution of finances directly to schools from central government, it was suggested, would enable schools to deflect monies that would otherwise be used to support SEN pupils to other aspects of school provision. And the introduction of league tables, based on the performance of schools across a very narrow range of indicators, was likely to mean that schools would be reluctant to enrol children with SEN for fear of their position in local league tables being compromised. It is arguably the last issue which has been the most controversial, ongoing and bitterly contested impact of the 1988 Act.

Discussion point/question: Are league tables a good way of ensuring that schools are accountable, or are they inconsistent with current developments towards 'inclusive education'?

Further reading

Slee, R. (2000) 'Talking back to power. The politics of educational exclusion'. International Special Education Congress. Manchester, 24–28 July.

See also: National Curriculum

UNITED NATIONS CONVENTION ON THE RIGHTS OF THE CHILD (1989)

The 1989 UN Convention on the Rights of the Child made an emphatic statement regarding the rights and entitlement of disabled children to be educated in **mainstream schools**. This was the first time that an international document, recognised by the majority of nations, had been developed regarding children with SEN and disabilities. Article 23 of the Convention states that a child should be educated in such a way that will allow that child to achieve the 'fullest possible social integration and individual development'. The UN Committee on the Rights of the Child has subsequently interpreted this as a goal for the educational inclusion of all children, irrespective of their level of learning difficulty.

Article 2 indicates that the content of the Convention shall apply to all children without discrimination – and it specifically mentions disability. Articles 3, 6, 12, 28 and 29 of the Convention give further support to the development of inclusive education for all disabled children. The UK ratified the Convention in 1991, thereby accepting responsibility for the obligations in it.

The UN Convention provided a major impetus for policy developments in many countries throughout the world, and should be viewed as the most crucial statement of international understanding of, and commitment to, SEN and disability. As such it has acted as a stimulus to many of the developments in this area in the English education system.

Discussion point/question: Some argue that some children have too many 'rights'. Is this a fair observation?

Further reading

Lundy, L. (2007) '"Voice" is not enough: Conceptualising Article 12 of the United Nations Convention on the Rights of the Child', *British Educational Research Journal*, 33(6), 927–42.

See also: children's rights; advocacy and empowerment; Children Act

CHILDREN ACT 1989

An increased focus on the rights and welfare of children was apparent throughout the 1980s. In England this process culminated in the

Children Act, which emphasised that the paramount consideration in a child's education and social upbringing is the child's welfare. The Act was built around a number of core principles which formed the basis of much subsequent child-protection legislation and the subsequent reshaped legislation of the Children Act in 2004. The Children Act was updated in 2004 to include provision for a children's commissioner and a requirement that local authorities make arrangements for collaboration between the range of professional agencies dealing with children and young people.

The Act stated that, wherever possible, children should be brought up and cared for within their own families. Where cases were identified in which a child had particular welfare needs, parents with such children should be helped to bring up their children themselves. This help would be provided as a service to the child and his or her family, and was intended to be provided in partnership with the parents. Emphasis was placed on the need to recognise differences in race, culture, religion and language in providing support. Moreover, the Act was highly proactive, stating that children should be safe and be protected by effective intervention if they are in danger, and that this should be undertaken swiftly through the courts.

Importantly, too, the Act required that the children are kept informed about what happens to them, and should participate when decisions are made about their future. Equally, parents would continue to have parental responsibility for their children, even when their children are no longer living with them. Like the child, they should participate in decision making concerning their child's welfare. A major strength of the Children Act, and a precursor to subsequent practices enshrined within the Children's Agenda, was the promotion of effective partnerships between the local authority and other agencies, including voluntary agencies.

Discussion point/question: All schools have a 'duty of care' towards their pupils. Does their responsibility towards SEN pupils in this respect present more of a challenge?

Further reading

Hendrick, H. (2005) *Child Welfare and Social Policy*. Bristol: The Policy Press.

See also: children's rights; advocacy and empowerment; United Nations Convention on the Rights of the Child

ELTON REPORT (1989)

The report of the Department of Education and Science's Committee of Enquiry chaired by Lord Elton was entitled *Discipline in Schools*. It was established to address concerns regarding so-called 'disruptive behaviour' in schools. Even though its recommendations are almost 20 years old, it remains an influential document concerning behaviour. Many of its findings heralded new ways in which behaviour by pupils (including those with SEN relating to emotional and behavioural difficulties) can best be managed. The report comprised 173 separate recommendations, many of which subsequently found their way into official government policy.

The report advocated a whole-school approach to pupil behaviour. It suggested that schools can best ensure that inappropriate behaviour is kept to a minimum by having an orderly and purposeful atmosphere and a set of working principles that are shared by all. It was recommended that this commitment to a sense of corporate responsibility and the development of a school-wide ethos of positive approaches to managing pupils was enshrined within a school policy which highlighted 'good behaviour' and a provision of appropriate rewards. Whilst the school policy should provide a framework through which pupils who misbehave could be sanctioned, the Committee's view was that a proactive and pre-emptive approach, rather than a punitive and reactive stance, was more likely to pay dividends. It suggested that schools set out a policy which included very explicit procedures for managing behaviour, including the process of rewards and sanctions. The policy also incorporated details of roles and responsibilities for managing behaviour.

The Elton Report was innovative in that it was one of the first official documents to make firm links between learning and behaviour. The report stated that everybody involved in the planning, delivery and evaluation of the curriculum should recognise that the quality of teaching and learning has a significant impact on pupils' behaviour.

The report did make recommendations regarding the need to focus on pupil behaviour during **initial teacher training**. The official response concerning this was for the government to make 'practical class management' a compulsory element in teacher training.

The validity of the findings of the Elton Report was enhanced because it was supported by a large-scale piece of commissioned research. This surveyed a representative sample of teachers from primary and secondary schools in England. Findings from this project indicated that less than 2 per cent of all staff surveyed were affected by serious physical aggression, whilst less than one in six of the teachers felt that discipline was a serious problem.

Discussion point/question: Research in the Elton Report suggested that problem behaviour by pupils in schools is not on the increase. Do you think this is still the case?

Further reading

Wheldall, K. (ed.) (1992). *Discipline in Schools: Psychological Perspectives on the Elton Report*. London: Routledge.

See also: emotional and behavioural difficulties; disruptive behaviour

SALAMANCA STATEMENT (1994)

In 1994 a world conference on special needs education took place in Salamanca, Spain. Almost 100 countries and many international organisations took part. A statement (subsequently referred to as the Salamanca Statement) was issued concerning the education of all disabled children. Delegates called for **inclusion** in **mainstream schools** of all children with SEN to become the universally accepted approach. The conference also proposed a framework for action which was underpinned by the principle that mainstream schools should accommodate all children, irrespective of their physical, intellectual, social, emotional, linguistic and other conditions. It also demanded that all educational policies should enable children to attend their local school, whether or not they had a disability.

The Salamanca Statement was influential because it was the product of an international agreement from representatives of 92 nations. As a collective they called on governments worldwide to address a number of vital issues for the further development of inclusive education. All governments should adopt the following.

- Give the 'highest policy and budgetary priority' to improve education services so that all children could be included, regardless of differences or difficulties.
- Adopt as a matter of law or policy the principle of inclusive education.
- Ensure that organisations of disabled people, along with parents and community bodies, are involved in planning decision making.

- Ensure that both **initial teacher training** and in- training address the provision of inclusive education.

The subsequent widespread publicity given to the Salamanca Statement acted as a stimulus to inclusive thinking in many countries, and greatly raised the profile of SEN in doing so.

Discussion point/question: Do you think that international agreements or resolutions, like the Salamanca Statement, have any real effect on the lives and outcomes of disabled children and young people?

Further reading

Vlachou, A. (1999). *Struggles for Inclusive Education*. Buckingham: Open University Press.

See also: inclusion

CODE OF PRACTICE (1994 AND 2001)

The SEN Code of Practice (2001) is the current document which sets out the practical guidance to school governing bodies, head teachers and teachers in general, as well as to other professions (including health and social services) involved in the provision of SEN services to children with learning difficulties. It is largely based on its predecessor, which was introduced in 1994 and which it supersedes. It is the statutory guidance which these groups have to take notice of in discharging their duties under Part IV of the **Education Act 1996**. The Code is directed to all maintained schools and settings in receipt of government funding, from nursery and early years provision to **mainstream** and **special school** settings.

The Code of Practice sets out a wide set of guidance regarding local authorities (LAs) and school-based policies and procedures aimed at enabling SEN pupils to reach their full potential both academically and socially, in order that they are more fully included in their school communities and subsequently able to make a successful transition to adulthood. The Code reinforces the now widely accepted view that the vast majority of children with SEN should be educated in mainstream schools, subject to certain arrangements being put in place by the school itself to ensure that their individual needs are met. It indicates that, for other children, additional help from SEN services

...s external to the school will be required. Often these ... be provided via the LA's **children's services** team. In ..., the Code states that a small minority of children will have ... SEN of a severity or complexity that requires the LA itself to determine and arrange specific SEN provision to cater for their learning difficulties.

The SEN Code of Practice recommends that schools adopt a 'graduated approach' to meeting children's SEN. It is here that the concepts of **School Action** (SA) and **School Action Plus** (SAP) were introduced in order to highlight the importance of initial intervention by teachers in the school (SA), prior to the involvement of external professionals (SAP).

The Code also provides both advice and the required protocols for conducting a statutory **assessment** of a child's SEN, and guidance for subsequently making and maintaining a **statement** of SEN for children with severe and complex educational needs. Information is also given regarding the conduct of statutory annual reviews of statements. Additional information is provided regarding the procedures for enabling young people with SEN to make the transition to college, training and employment.

Finally, the 2001 Code of Practice emphasises the importance of involving children and parents in decision making and of effective multi-agency working to combine services around the needs of the child with SEN and their families.

The Code provides an 'SEN tool kit' for teachers and other professionals, to support them in discharging their responsibilities to pupils with SEN. It provides advice and suggests different kinds of action that schools might take to support children with SEN.

Discussion point/question: The SEN Code of Practice is the responsibility of all teachers. Do you think that this is realistic, given that some teachers may not be too interested in learners who experience difficulties?

Further reading

Cowne, E. (2005) 'What do special educational needs coordinators think they do?', *Support for Learning*, 20(2), 61–8.

See also: special needs coordinator; class teacher

EDUCATION ACT 1996

The Education Act 1996 was important in that, although it made few changes to the existing law on special education, it performed the function of acting as a means of synthesising what had gone before. In doing this it ensured that certain key elements of existing legislation were highlighted or strengthened. Thus, it incorporated changes made by the Disability Discrimination Act 1995, the amended Education Act 1993 and the Nursery Education and Grant-Maintained Schools Act 1996 and enabled these various changes in both nuance and substance to be located in a single piece of legislation.

In summary, the most important features of the 1996 Act were as follows.

- A separate 'code of practice' giving detailed practical guidance to schools and local authorities (LAs) on how to meet the needs of pupils with SEN.
- A limit of 26 weeks to complete the legal process for identifying and assessing SEN and, where appropriate, issuing a legally binding **statement** of SEN.
- Parents of children with statements would be able to say which **mainstream school** they wished their child to attend.
- Duties on schools to draw up, publish, and report on their SEN policy.
- Parents' rights of appeal against LA decisions were strengthened with the establishment of an independent **SEN Tribunal**.

Discussion point/question: Why should a limit be placed on the amount of time taken to identify, assess and provide a statement of educational need for an SEN child?

Further reading

Kirby, A. (2006) *Mapping SEN Routes through Identification to Intervention.* London: David Fulton.

See also: statement of SEN; SEN Tribunal

GREEN PAPER (1997) AND PROGRAMME OF ACTION (1998)

The 1997 Green Paper was entitled *Excellence for all Children: Meeting Special Educational Need*. It set out six key themes for SEN development in schools, and in doing so gave an indication of the range and extent of changes that were likely to be set in place in SEN over the next five or more years. Amongst the Green Paper's proposals was the introduction of strategies relating to setting high expectations for children with SEN, supporting parents of children with SEN and promoting **inclusion**.

The overarching principle was that of inclusion. As Beveridge (1999) comments, 'The Green Paper (1997) provides a strong endorsement of the principles of inclusion on moral and social as well as educational grounds'. This signalled the intention of government to encourage **mainstream schools** to address an even wider and more complex range of learning difficulties than they hitherto had done. It also placed a new emphasis on the **class teacher**'s role as the starting point in meeting the needs of children with SEN, recognising that this kind of **early intervention** is 'the best way to tackle educational disadvantage'.

Subsequently, the government announced its operational strategy to put into practice the Green Paper thinking. In 1998, therefore, *Meeting Special Educational Needs: A Programme of Action* was introduced, and it sought to provide a set of key aims. It did this under five themes:

1. Working with parents. Plans include:

   - provision of high-quality **early years education**;
   - early identification of learning difficulties;
   - introduction of parent partnership schemes;
   - introduction of conciliation arrangements for disputes;
   - more involvement of children in the process.

2. Improving the SEN framework. Plans include:

   - introduction of a simplified code of practice in 2000/2001;
   - introduction of guidance on the placement of children;
   - more local education authority (LEA) accountability (publishing of LEA plans for SEN);
   - improvements to the **SEN Tribunal**.

3. Developing inclusive systems. Plans include:

- LEAs to publish inclusion arrangements;
- review of statutory framework for **inclusion**;
- links between special and mainstream schools;
- fair treatment of SEN children in the admissions process;
- financial support for inclusion projects.

4. Developing knowledge and skills. Plans include:

- greater emphasis on SEN in teacher training;
- publish 'good-practice' guides for learning support assistants;
- consultation on the future role of the educational psychologist;
- professional development for teachers working in SEN.

5. Working in partnership. Plans include:

- extended regional coordination of SEN provision;
- introduction of new duties of partnership (e.g. with the NHS);
- developments in speech and language service;
- more focus on 16+ provision.

The *Programme of Action* was to become the basis for government SEN policy for five years, and formed the context for such important initiatives as the Children Agenda and **Every Child Matters**.

Discussion point/question: Why has it become increasingly important for government to adopt an inter-service, coordinated approach to policy in SEN?

Further reading

Wearmouth J. (2001) *Special Educational Provision: Meeting the Challenge in Schools*. London: Hodder and Stoughton.

See also: Every Child Matters

INCLUSIVE SCHOOLING (2001) (DFES)

The document *Inclusive Schooling: Children with Special Educational Needs* (DfES, 2001) provides statutory guidance regarding the practical operation of the new statutory framework for inclusive education contained in the **Education Act 1996**. The guidance sets out a series of principles on which inclusive educational services for children should be based. These include commitments to the following beliefs.

- Most children with special educational needs can be successfully included in **mainstream education**, providing staff receive appropriate training, strategies and support.
- An inclusive education service should offer excellence and choice, and provide opportunities for the views of parents and children to be heard.
- Schools, local authorities (LAs) and others should actively seek to remove barriers to learning and participation.
- Mainstream education will not always be appropriate for every child throughout their compulsory years of schooling.

Informed by these principles, *Inclusive Schooling* deals with a range of issues which the government of the day regarded as central to the development of effective inclusion in schools. Thus, it addressed such issues as the development of effective inclusion strategies in schools, disability equality, pupil voice, partnerships with parents and the topical question of safeguarding the needs of pupils with SEN.

The document also considered how inter-agency partnerships could best promote inclusion, as well as the problematic issues of parental choice/preference in school selection for their SEN child. In the case of the latter, it discusses procedures in cases where it may not be possible to include certain children who have **statements** of SEN in mainstream schools.

Whilst, in general terms, the document was well received, and was viewed as a signal of government's intention to support further development and resourcing of SEN and inclusive education, there was some concern expressed regarding at least one aspect of the guidance. Thus, *Inclusive Schooling* offers guidance to both LAs and to schools to enable them to 'ensure that a child's inclusion is not incompatible with the efficient education of other children'. This was interpreted to mean that SEN was unlikely to be a priority in many schools, as it could be argued that the resource-intensive nature of SEN support would be viewed as depriving other pupils of resources. There would always be a justifiable argument, it was claimed, for not allocating resources to SEN pupils because it ran contrary to the principle of 'efficient' education.

Discussion point/question: Is the concept of inclusive education purely an ethical and moral issue? Should practical issues (like resources, financial issues and so on) be part of a debate regarding its efficacy?

Further reading

Thomas, G., Walker, D. and Webb, J. (1998) *The Making of the Inclusive School*. London: Routledge.

See also: inclusion and individual rights; Salamanca Statement

SPECIAL EDUCATIONAL NEEDS AND DISABILITY ACT 2003

The Special Educational Needs and Disability Act (SENDA) 2001 introduced some important changes in the provision for pupils with SEN and disabilities. The Act affects all aspects of educational provision, from nurseries through to higher education.

The first part of the Act emphatically stated that it was the parent's right to have their child educated in a mainstream setting, irrespective of the level of disability or SEN. The subsequent document *Inclusive Schooling: Children with Special Educational Needs*, published by government in 2001, gives guidance on how this approach could be made concrete. Importantly, it ensures that a 'get-out' clause in earlier legislation (which prevented inclusion in mainstream schools of an SEN pupil if this was 'incompatible with the efficient education of other children') was removed. A number of examples of the 'reasonable steps' schools and other settings might take to include children with SEN were also provided.

The SENDA Act 2001 also strengthened the requirement that schools should inform parents when they make special educational provision because they have identified their child as having SEN, whilst also permitting schools to request a statutory assessment of a pupil in the same way that parents can. Other aspects of revision or innovation included the requirement that local authorities (LAs) advertise parent partnership services and also that they set up systems for resolving disagreements between parents and schools and between parents and the LA.

Disability discrimination in schools and other educational settings was the second focus of the Act. The contents of the Act seek to ensure that disabled pupils are not discriminated against in any aspect of school life in that it 'makes it unlawful to discriminate against disabled pupils and prospective pupils in admissions, in education and associated services and in exclusions'.

In meeting this requirement, the Act sets out a duty on schools not to treat disabled pupils less favourably than other (non-disabled) pupils. In particular, it laid out requirements for all LAs and schools to make adaptations to their physical environment (classrooms, corridors, social areas including playgrounds) to ensure that disabled pupils could access them freely. And the Act also required schools to ensure that disabled pupils had full access to the curriculum. The whole process was to be overseen and reported on by the Office for Standards in Education, Children's Services and Skills (Ofsted).

Discussion point/question: Can you list some of the 'reasonable steps' that might be undertaken to make a learning environment which you are familiar with more accessible to disabled learners?

Further reading

Banks, P., Cogan, N., Deeley, S., Hill, M., Riddell, S. and Tisdall, K. (2001) 'Seeing the invisible: Children and young people affected by disability', *Disability & Society,* 16(6), 797–814.

See also: children's rights

EVERY CHILD MATTERS (2004)

This legislation represents a major national strategic initiative designed to improve the services provided to children and families. The Every Child Matters (ECM) agenda is delivered through integrated children's services which form a **'team around the child'**, and has its focus within schools and communities. ECM identifies a set of five areas of activity in supporting children:

- being healthy
- staying safe
- enjoying and achieving
- making a positive contribution
- economic well-being.

Each of these are described through sets of aims, targets, indicators and inspection criteria. They are key elements in the activities of the newly established **children's services**, which combine former local education authorities, social services departments and, in many cases, child health services. New local authority inspections – Joint Area

Reviews – will inspect this service and base judgements on the extent to which they are having a positive impact on the lives of children. Needless to say, these new arrangements have had major implications for all professional groups working with children and families, and have been a confirmation of, and a catalyst for, professional collaboration.

Discussion point/question: Which of the five strands of the *Every Child Matters* agenda would you regard as the most important? Debate your views with a fellow student or colleague.

Further reading

Cheminais, R. (2006) *Every Child Matters. A Practical Guide for Teachers.* London: David Fulton.

See also: Green Paper and Programme for Action; Children's Plan

CHILDREN'S PLAN (2007)

The Department for Children, Schools and Families (DCSF) published a ten-year strategy, *The Children's Plan: Building Brighter Futures*, late in 2007. As with many documents from central government in England, the proposals it contains have significance for SEN, even though it is directed towards generic education provision. The Plan outlines the government's strategy to further improve the lives of children and young people, and is backed by £1 billion of planned spending between 2008 and 2012.

The main proposals within the Plan which will have the most significant impact on SEN provision relate to the following:

- Strengthening support for all families during the early years of their children's lives – a key point for intervention with children with learning difficulties.
- Reviewing **child and adolescent mental health service** provision for children and young people with mental health issues.
- Ensuring that nurseries in the most disadvantaged areas have at least two graduate-qualified employees by 2015.
- Providing 12,000 two-year olds from disadvantaged families with free childcare over the next three years.
- The allocation of £25 million to fund the Every Child a Writer scheme, in addition to the £144 million allocated to fund the

Every Child a Reader and Every Child Counts programmes – thus providing support to SEN children with learning difficulties in these areas of the curriculum.

- Ensuring that parents receive up-to-date information about their child's progress, attendance and behaviour – the latter is a key aspect of dealing with unacceptable behaviour in school.
- A commitment to improve **initial teacher training** in SEN by providing funding of £18 million over three years between 2008 and 2011.
- A review by Ofsted into SEN provision in 2009.
- Greater regulation of **pupil referral units**.
- The allocation of £66 million over the three years to support young people most at risk of getting into crime.
- Supporting young carers and deliver new support for families with disabled children.

As might be gathered from these SEN-related extracts from the Children's Plan, the initiative is characterised by an interdepartmental, multi-agency approach which is consistent with the policy orientations of the last ten years in SEN. Schools and teachers are no longer seen as solely responsible for the educational and social achievement of children, particularly so when a child has an SEN. The Children's Plan represents an ambitious commitment to take action in education, health, social care, community affairs, juvenile justice, recreation and housing. Whether the ambitions will be realised in the face of competing economic pressures and changing political dimensions remains very much to be seen.

Discussion point/question: Claims have been made that legislation like the Children's Plan is too cumbersome and bureaucratic. Is such a wide-ranging, interdisciplinary policy necessary for the well-being of children with SEN?

Further reading

Vincent, C. and Ball, S. (2005) 'The 'childcare champion'?: New Labour, social justice and the childcare market', *British Educational Research Journal*, 31(5), 557–70.

See also: child and adolescent mental health services; team around the child; extended schools

BERCOW REPORT (2008)

The Bercow Report (2008) was the product of an independent review of services for children and young people with speech, language and communication needs commissioned by the UK government. It was the first major review of this kind for seven years in an aspect of SEN which was increasingly viewed as affecting an increasing number of vulnerable children and young people.

The report emphasises the importance of enabling children to develop the skills and confidence to communicate. This, the report suggests, is an essential life skill for all children and young people, and is crucial to their social, emotional and educational development. And yet the members of the team compiling the report point to evidence of insufficient understanding of the importance of speech, language and communication amongst policy makers, professionals and service providers, and sometimes even parents and families.

The report makes 40 recommendations which are gathered under five themes.

- Communication is crucial.
- Early **identification** and intervention are essential.
- A continuum of services designed around the family is needed.
- Joint working is critical.
- The current system is characterised by high variability and a lack of equity.

Amongst the recommendations are that more focus is placed on training speech, language and communication specialists, and that it receives far more emphasis at both primary and secondary school levels. Moreover, the report recommends that government 'reinforces its inclusive approach to SEN in the newly revised secondary curriculum by preparing and disseminating widely exemplifications of the effective removal of barriers for pupils with SLCN [speech, language and communication needs], in line with the principles of the National Curriculum inclusion statement'.

There is an emphasis on the development of effective communication for *all* children in the report, as it is a core aspect of building effective relationships. If children and young people can communicate effectively, using a wide repertoire, they are less likely to become frustrated about a perceived inequality or grievance. 'Listening schools' and 'listening classrooms' can thrive only where all pupils have the skills and strategies to communicate. Moreover, many of the recommendations made are consistent with the overall approaches adopted by the **social and emotional aspects of learning** strategies in primary and secondary settings.

Discussion point/question: The Bercow Report comes only a few years after the inception of the **National Literacy Strategy** (which included an emphasis on 'speaking and listening'). Why is it that such a great amount of attention is being directed towards developing communication skills in children and young people?

Further reading

Asprey, A. and Nash, T. (2006) 'The importance of awareness and communication for the inclusion of young people with life-limiting and life-threatening conditions in mainstream schools and colleges', *British Journal of Special Education*, 33(1), 10–18.

See also: speech and language disorder

PRACTICE AND PROVISION

ART THERAPY

Art is a valuable educational activity in its own right, and apart from its aesthetic and recreational values, it also enables children to pull together a range of their thoughts, experiences and reflections in the construction of a creative object. to make a new and meaningful whole. Art is vitally important to children's development. It is one of the first ways in which a child interacts with the environment, gaining understanding as this is done. In other words, it is a 'way in' to the complex, often confusing world which is mainly adult dominated. Making a painting or drawing, or any other art object, is also one of the first opportunities for the child to express their individuality. It thus comprises a very intuitive and powerful means through which the child can communicate. Given that art enables the child to develop self-expression, it ensures that what is represented, in whatever medium, is individual to the child.

In cases where a child's normal psychological and social development has been interrupted – for instance, by illness, trauma or a learning disability – the use of art can allow the child to say things which they might feel unable to say in other ways. Not only can art function as a means through which the child can understand the origin of a difficulty being encountered; it also can lead to a greater sense of control and empowerment, allowing the child to move forward.

Art therapy is an approach which has been used over many years as a means of enabling children with SEN to gain greater insights into themselves as individual learners. It comprises a combination of the disciplines of art and therapy. The word 'therapy' originated from the Greek, and means, broadly speaking, 'meeting the needs of another'. Frequently art is used as a therapeutic device in cases where the child has been identified as experiencing emotional, social or behavioural difficulties. It can also be used to foster a child's motor skills, assisting with both fine and gross motor control. An art therapy session provides an opportunity for a child who experiences SEN to have focused attention in order to address their identified needs. The art created can constitute a cathartic process in its own right. But it can also be used as a vehicle to promote conversation about the personal meanings of the images created. The art therapist's role is to provide practical help and assistance with the materials and technical help to the child regarding the medium that is being used. The therapist will offer encouragement to the child and to enable new possibilities and understandings to be drawn from what has been produced.

Of course, art is often used informally in education as a means through which children can express their feelings. The work of Rudolf Steiner (1861–1925) is important in this respect. Steiner was an Austrian philosopher, literary scholar, educator and artist. His ideas were incorporated into the Steiner–Waldorf education movement, which emphasises that learning is interdisciplinary, combining practical, artistic and intellectual elements. There are numerous Steiner schools in the UK and worldwide; many provide an 'alternative' curriculum which is viewed by some as being more able to meet the needs of children who have SEN.

The profession of art therapy has developed considerably in recent years and now several universities and colleges provide training courses in art therapy. Such courses often cover a wide range of themes. Typically they will explore the psychology of marks and symbols, non-verbal communication, the psychotherapeutic aspects of child development, family dynamics and social interaction. This is all premised on the notion that creative images constitute a very important means of human communication and are extremely powerful in helping children (and adults) to verbalise things that they often find difficult to explain.

Discussion point/question: Can you think of any ethical issues regarding the role of art in a therapeutic context with children with SEN?

Further reading

Hagood, M. (2001) *The Use of Art in Counselling Child and Adult Survivors of Sexual Abuse*. London: Jessica Kingsley.

See also: social and emotional aspect of learning

ASSISTIVE TECHNOLOGY

The term 'assistive technology' is now widely used to describe how educationists make use of technology, including computers, to enable the learning environment (especially including the curriculum) to be more accessible to those pupils who have SEN. Indeed, 'assistive technology' has been described by Professor Stephen Hawking, a famous assistive-technology user, as 'a bridge to independence'.

In just the same way that the computer has revolutionised the way that we work and play, so too has it had a dramatic and highly visible effect on learning in schools. Nowhere has this been more apparent than in the case of children who experience SEN. During that time, the computer has become indispensable to teachers and others who work with children who have severe learning difficulties. The advent of more powerful processors has enabled manufacturers to develop more and more sophisticated hardware and software, which has enabled pupils with SEN to obtain greater access to both the formal curriculum and the social, or so-called 'hidden', curriculum.

Computers and other assistive technology in school enable children to gain in self-confidence and to develop social and communication skills. Their use can also support the development of important gross and fine motor skills. For example, the child who has a physical disability and who, in consequence, is unable to hold a pencil can use graphics programmes for drawing and word processors for writing. Children who, like Hawking himself, are unable to speak can use assistive technology as a communication tool. It could therefore be stated that these technological approaches are a vital way of supporting the greater inclusion of SEN pupils in mainstream classrooms.

Like all other children, learners who have particular SEN, including those with restricted vision, poor motor control or difficulty in reading or processing language, can benefit from using a computer and other technologies. Developments in the last 20 years have ensured that even those pupils with severe SEN can now make use of technology to support their learning.

For some learners, whose SEN are less pronounced, simple adjustments to the accessibility option of a learning package will be all that is required. This might include changing the size of the text or the background colours so that the screen images are easier to see. Other pupils, however, will require greater adaptations. This may involve providing them with technical support so that they are able to use a standard keyboard; for example, a keyboard overlay or a software package that will convert on-screen text to speech.

Discussion point/question: How best can schools and teachers keep abreast of the rapid developments in information and communication technology, in order to ensure that SEN pupils are supported by the latest software and hardware?

Further reading

Florian, L. and Hegarty, S. (2004) *ICT and Special Educational Needs: A Tool for Inclusion*. Buckingham: Open University Press.

See also: differentiation

BEHAVIOUR FOR LEARNING

The concept that the behaviour of children in school is directly linked to their learning has been around for some time. When pupils are interested and engaged during a lesson they are less likely to present SEN associated with **emotional and behavioural difficulties** (EBDs). There has been considerable renewed focus on this idea, beginning with a meta-analysis of research papers concerning how theories of behaviour helped inform teaching strategies (Powell and Tod, 2004). This suggested that, in order for children to learn effectively and behave according to accepted classroom rules, three sets of relationships had to be in place: the child's 'relationship' with himself or herself and with 'others' (pupils, teachers and other adults), and his or her relationship with the curriculum itself.

The theory of 'behaviour for learning' is based on this triumvirate of relationships, and suggests that unless there is a positive equilibrium in each relationship area, the child's learning *and* his or her behaviour will tend to present challenges. Moreover, the theory is consistent with the views presented in the national behaviour and attendance strategies. These suggest that, whilst unacceptable behaviour should never be condoned and always dealt with, the emphasis should be on promoting positive behaviour.

The Behaviour for Learning (B4L) approach was used as the basis for a major initiative in teacher education in the area of special emotional and behavioural difficulties. Starting in 2004, the B4L initiative was launched as an electronic, web-based resource for trainee teachers and their tutors. This was in response to successive national surveys of those completing their teacher training, in which many expressed a view that training in the area of pupil behaviour was unsatisfactory, or, at best, average.

Subsequently the B4L initiative has become widely used as a practical resource and a reference point. On average over 2500 users download materials from its pages every day and the resource provides links to a range of SEN-related materials in the area of EBDs.

Discussion point/question: Do *you* think that behaviour and learning are linked? Can you recall an occasion when you were not stimulated by a particular lesson? What was your response?

Further reading

Powell, S. and Tod, J. (2004) *A Systematic Review Of How Theories Explain Learning Behaviour in School Contexts*. London: EPPI-Centre, SSRU.

See also: disruptive behaviour; social and emotional aspects of learning; emotional and behavioural difficulties; delinquency; exclusions

BEHAVIOUR MODIFICATION

Behaviour modification refers to the alteration of a child's behaviour using basic learning techniques and positive or negative reinforcement (as in rewards and punishments). The core premise of the approach is that all behaviour is learned, and therefore it can be unlearned. Variations of the approach are widely used in schools, although behaviour modification had its origins in the institutional treatment of human behavioural disorders through the reinforcement of acceptable behaviour and the reduction (or suppression) of unwanted behaviours.

Behaviour modification has its origins in the work of Ivan Pavlov, a Russian physiologist who observed that animals could be taught to respond to stimuli that might otherwise have no effect on them. In the USA, B.F. Skinner further developed the technique, using positive or negative 'reinforcers' to encourage desirable behaviour and punishments and to discourage undesirable behaviour. Behaviour modification focuses very much on observed, identifiable behaviours. It does not seek to address the basic causes of a behaviour (although it may use knowledge of these to determine what positive or negative reinforcements are used in an intervention programme. Thus the approach has little to do with the subliminal or unconscious aspects of a child's personality – an issue which has resulted in behaviour modification being criticised on account of its failure to take account of the wishes or experiences of the child.

Behaviour modification techniques are characterised by an emphasis on describing the child's behaviour in measurable terms, using techniques that can also be described accurately and applied systematically. The technique is, as stated earlier, based on the principles of learning and there is a strong emphasis on intervention 'measurement', in order to scientifically demonstrate that a particular technique was responsible for a particular behaviour change.

The use of behaviour modification, although it has been criticised by some on account of its failure to take the 'whole child' into account, is nevertheless in widespread use in SEN in the UK. It is used as the basis for intervention in cases where children experience special **emotional and behavioural difficulties, attention deficit (hyperactivity) disorder** and several other distinctive SEN (for example, **autistic** spectrum disorders). A typical approach would require a teacher to firstly define the 'problem' presented by the pupil. This is usually done by using an observation schedule so that the most frequent or serious behaviour is identified. The teacher will next design a programme to 'modify' the unwanted behaviour. This will involve the use of a 'reinforcer', which is applied in order to change the target behaviour.

The underlying principles of behaviour modification now inform many of the ways that teachers manage individual pupils or even whole classes. Such techniques as the use of social praise, tokens as rewards and 'time out' are all based on the psychological premise of behaviour modification.

Discussion point/question: To what extent is it the case that behaviour can change only with the approval and informed consent of the child or young person? Does this raise ethical issues for the teacher?

Further reading

Cooper, P., Smith, C. and Upton, G. (1994) *Emotional Behavioural Difficulties: Theory to Practice*. London: Routledge.

See also: emotional and behavioural difficulties

CASE CONFERENCE

Case conferences are convened periodically to review the progress a child with an identified SEN is making against a set of targets (usually contained in an individual education plan). They also provide the important function of assisting in the planning of future work with the child and of sharing new information. Case conferences are attended by a wide range of stakeholders. They may involve parents or carers, the young person with SEN, the **special needs coordinator** and other teachers, as well as professionals involved in the case (for example, the **educational psychologist**, **occupational therapist** or social worker). For children and young people with a '**statement** of SEN', case conferences which focus on an annual review of progress are an essential part of a professional response to that child's needs.

It is possible that a number of case conferences can take place relating to an individual child in any given school year. This will depend on the nature of the SEN, disabilities or other issues which the child is experiencing. For example, if the child is regarded as being 'at risk' of harm or abuse, they may be the subject of a child protection case conference. Similarly, a case conference may be required where there is a planned move between one stage in the child's education to another, a process called 'transition planning'. And the recent move towards building a '**team around the child**' will require a similar arrangement, so that a range of stakeholders can examine the existing provision for the child and set future targets.

Discussion point/question: Do you think that some parents might be reluctant to attend a case conference because they feel deskilled in the presence of childcare and education professionals? What can be done about such situations?

Further reading

Wolfendale, S. (1999) 'Parents as partners in research and evaluation: Methodological and ethical issues and solutions', *British Journal of Special Education*, 26(3), 164–9.

See also: educational psychologist; occupational therapist; special needs coordinator

CHILDREN'S SERVICES

An improved partnership approach – in which services working together to meet the SEN of children and the needs of families – has been a major feature of both policy and practice in special education since the publication of **Every Child Matters** in 1998. Even prior to this there was much evidence of individual local authority services working together on SEN matters; indeed, this approach was recommended in the **Warnock Report (1978)** itself. There was, therefore, a sound base for developing integrated local services delivery and good inter-agency links.

From 1998 all those groups involved with providing services to children, ranging from hospitals and schools to police and voluntary groups, started to work in an even more sophisticated and collaborative way. This way of working, apart from its intrinsic worth in enabling more efficient cooperation to support children and young people, was also prompted by the earlier findings of public enquiries into a number of high-profile cases of child abuse. In these it was clear that lack of collaboration between different services had resulted in important information being lost and with it the opportunity to protect a child from serious harm. Given that there are now so many different agencies and services for children, it was viewed as essential that all these needed a strategic and coordinated approach – especially given that many of the children most likely to be involved were 'at risk' on account of their SEN.

The relatively recent emergence of children's services has brought significant benefits. For example, teachers working with the **child and adolescent mental health services** have noted an increase in children's happiness and well-being and a measurable improvement in children's behaviour. Improved academic attainment in the same group has also been apparent. In the case of disabled children, families who have 'key workers' to coordinate services have reported improvements in their quality of life, more satisfying and productive relationships with services, quicker access to services and reduced levels of stress (Sloper, 2004).

Related to the work of children's services in local authorities, in 2005 the government appointed the first Children's Commissioner for England. The Commissioner acts as a figurehead and spokesperson, giving children and young people a voice in government and in public life. In undertaking this role, particular attention is given to gathering and expressing the views of the most vulnerable children and young people in society, including those with SEN.

Discussion point/question: Why do 'children' require specific service arrangements, as compared (for example) to adults? What benefits are likely for SEN pupils?

Further reading

Sloper, P. (2004) 'Facilitators and barriers for coordinated multi-agency services', *Child Care, Health and Development*, 30(6), 571–80.

See also: support services; professional support; professional collaboration

CONDUCTIVE EDUCATION

Conductive education is an education system for children with motor disorders. One of the major consequences of this disorder is that children have difficulty in controlling their body movements. There are several causes for the physical difficulties that these children experience, and there is a range of resulting diseases, syndromes and ensuing learning difficulties. They can be the result of disease or damage to the central nervous system resulting in (for example) cerebral palsy, Parkinson's disease, dyspraxia and multiple sclerosis, as well as other motor problems which have a neurological origin.

The origins of conductive pedagogy are not known, although there is a consensus view that it is largely based on the professional practice of Austrian-Hungarian physician András Pető, who worked as a doctor in and around Vienna during the Second World War and who proposed the strategy of early 'movement therapy'. Following the war Pető moved to Hungary, where, under the patronage of the government, he established the Pető Institute, which was both a school and a provider of professional training. Subsequently 'Peto centres' were established in many countries, mainly in post-industrial settings where financial resources to support educational innovations of this kind were available.

Conductive education, as the name implies, is an educational approach which provides support to children with motor disabilities, aiming to enable them to live an independent and active life. It is based on conventional 'learning theory' and an underlying assumption that all children are capable of learning if appropriately taught.

It is a process that allows children to improve their motor control by providing them with the opportunity to develop the best 'pathways' from the brain to the body. This is accomplished by supporting the child to attain a series of short-term, achievable goals.

Discussion point/question: Because of the regularity and timing of daily interventions, is a conductive education strategy viable only in non-mainstream contexts?

Further reading

Lambert, M. (2005) 'Conductive education: Links with mainstream schools', *Support for Learning*, 19(1), 31–7.

See also: multi-sensory approaches; sensory and/or physical

DIAGNOSTIC TESTING

Diagnostic tests are those conducted to provide **class teachers**, **educational psychologists** and related educational professions with detailed information regarding the capabilities and learning difficulties of the child experiencing SEN. Of course, diagnostic tests are widely used across education in general, and those generic tests will themselves provide an initial indication of the areas of need being experienced by a pupil in school. However, many generic-testing approaches function solely as 'standardised' or 'criterion-referenced' tests. These give fewer clues as to what lies behind the failure of a child to perform well in particular aspects of the curriculum.

Discussion point/question: What are the advantages of diagnostic tests? What part do they play in meeting the learning needs of pupils?

Further reading

Freeman, L. and Miller, A. (2001) 'Norm-referenced, criterion-referenced, and dynamic assessment: What exactly is the point?', *Educational Psychology in Practice*, 17(1), 3–16.

See also: class teacher, educational psychologist

DIFFERENTIATION

Differentiation of the curriculum represents the baseline strategy for dealing with an identified SEN. The approach has been defined as 'teaching things differently according to observed differences among learners' (Westwood, 2006). It is important to note that differentiation in the curriculum is one of the bases of effective generalist teaching. Whilst it has assumed significant importance in SEN, it remains applicable across the entire curriculum and at every level of the achievement spectrum. Fundamentally, therefore, it represents a recognition that learners are individuals. It is derived from a number of pedagogical approaches, notably those of task analysis, curriculum monitoring and review, pupil grouping, and learning and teaching styles. Whilst differentiation is a relatively straightforward term to define, most teachers will agree that, because it relates to an input–process–output model of teaching, it is not easy to put into practice.

A major reason for this is the time that it takes for a teacher to adapt teaching materials so that they are tailored to individual needs.

The first (input) stage in planning a differentiated approach is to focus on the content of what is going to be taught. This has to be matched to the aptitudes and capabilities of the learner, and is obviously heavily reliant on there being a suitable and accurate base-line **assessment**. This will tell the teacher what level of achievement the pupil is operating at and, consequently, how best to choose the content. But choice of materials is not the only consideration. Thought needs to be given to the interests of the pupil; this is particularly so where pupils have SEN relating to disaffection or off-task behaviour.

The planning stage needs also to take account of the use of resources. The teacher should endeavour to find material which the pupil will find stimulating and motivating, and which, perhaps, addresses the topic to be learnt in a way which enables the pupil to begin to 'scaffold' their learning so that one piece of information is seen to 'fit' with what follows. The planning stage will also involve considering how any additional support (whether from the child's peers or from other adults in the classroom) is to be utilised, as well as establishing how the lesson is to be divided into manageable chunks of time in order that the child's attention and motivation is kept.

A second element in differentiation concerns the process of learning and teaching. This is sometimes referred to as 'differentiation by process'. It involves putting into practice many of the issues considered in the planning stage, and places particular emphasis on differences in teaching and learning styles. Attention is therefore directed to such things as the balance between the different tasks and activities which comprise the whole lesson (some tasks might be structured group activities, others may be individual tasks and so on). Moreover, the teacher needs to take account of the differences in language and comprehension in the class – one of the frequent criticisms of underachieving children is that they 'didn't understand the teacher'. Moreover, the teacher should provide adequate opportunities for reinforcement, and summaries of what has been achieved during the lesson.

Third, differentiation can occur as a set of outcomes which allows pupils with different aptitudes and preferences to communicate their learning mastery in a range of ways. Pupils with SEN sometimes have great difficulty with **handwriting**, for example. In such cases the teacher should look for alternative ways in which the child can provide evidence of engagement with the learning task – by role play, video, or using illustration.

Discussion point/question: Does the task of making every lesson a series of differentiated tasks place an unmanageable burden on the class teacher? How has this issue been resolved in schools?

Further reading

McNamara, S. and Moreton, G. (1997) *Understanding Differentiation*. London: David Fulton.

See also: inclusion and individual rights; identification and assessment; National Curriculum

DRAMA THERAPY

Drama therapy has its origins in the healing rituals and dramas of various historical societies. In fact, Aristotle first used the term 'catharsis', an expression closely related to the intended outcomes of drama therapy whereby a new meaning or understanding is derived as a result of the intervention. Drama therapy has also been influenced by a range of other therapeutic approaches, including family therapy, gestalt therapy and systems theory. In its use of role play and the child's imagination, drama therapy has many affiliations with play therapy, which has become increasingly influential as the UK government has sought to place emphasis on the holistic development of children in the 'Foundation Stage' curriculum. It is important to note the strong relationships that have existed between drama therapy and play – some theorists believe that play marks the beginning of dramatic activity, whilst both Melanie Klein and D.W. Winnicott, two well-known psychotherapists who worked mainly with children, both noted the links between creativity, play and drama.

As with **art therapy**, drama therapy is used widely within special education, and is especially valuable in allowing children who may have communication difficulties, social interaction problems or **behaviour difficulties** to express themselves in a creative yet secure environment.

Of course, drama can also be used by teachers to enable them to build pupil confidence and self-esteem, and by giving them another vehicle to express themselves. Drama, used in this way in **mainstream school** settings, with groups of children including those with

SEN, can also encourage children to find new ways of thinking about their learning.

There are currently four postgraduate training courses in drama therapy in the UK. Those that lead to a qualification approved by the Health Professions Council are recognised by the Department of Health.

Discussion point/question: Can 'acting out' scenarios, which children might find challenging, help them to understand their responses if they were to encounter these scenarios in reality? Is 'role play' a useful aid for teachers working with SEN pupils?

Further reading

Cooper, C. (2004) '"A struggle well worth having": The uses of theatre-in-education (TIE) for learning', *Support for Learning*, 19(2), 81–7.

See also: art therapy; social and emotional aspects of learning; multi-sensory approaches

EARLY INTERVENTION

Early intervention has long been regarded as the most important element in securing learner progress. From the very beginnings of the development of SEN teaching, research and practice has highlighted the benefits to be gained by identifying SEN at an early stage and formulating a strategy to help remediate it.

Early intervention strategies are invoked well before a child attends school. Paediatricians and health visitors are amongst the first to assess the developmental progress of a baby, and will usually recognise early signals of potential concern if developmental milestones are not met. Parents, of course, have a vital role to play in this process. One of the key **National Strategies** to ensure that there is a coordinated approach during the earliest stages of a child's development is Sure Start. This provides a framework within which a range of professionals can work with parents and children to promote the physical, intellectual and social development of preschool children to ensure they are ready to learn on entry to school. Sure Start greatly increases the prospects of identifying children at risk of developing SEN because of its multidisciplinary approach. Once identified, the Sure Start team can then provide appropriate early intervention and support.

But sometimes a special educational need is not recognised prior to a child enrolling in primary school. At this stage the school's own assessment procedures come into operation. On entry all children will normally be screened in order to assess their levels of literacy and numeracy. Teachers will also have liaised with nursery settings, and will undertake observations during the initial months that the child is at school. Liaison with parents is another important part of this process. All these processes enable teachers to build up a picture of the level at which the child is operating and to put in place initial strategies, with the support of the school's **special educational needs coordinator** if any SEN are beginning to be manifest.

Discussion point/question: What might a teacher be 'looking for' when attempting to assess a child's early learning?

Further reading

Connor, M. (1998) 'A review of behavioural early intervention programmes for children with autism', *Educational Psychology in Practice*, 14, 109–117.

See also: diagnostic testing; early years education

EARLY YEARS EDUCATION

The UK government's current approach to SEN in the early years was launched in February 2004. It sets out plans to enable children with SEN to fulfil their potential. The government also announced a programme of subsequent action and review to support early years settings, schools and local authorities in their work for children with SEN. It does this in four key areas:

- emphasising early intervention – ensuring that children who have SEN receive help as soon as possible;
- removing barriers to learning – further developing inclusive practice in every early years setting;
- raising expectations and achievement – developing teachers' skills and strategies for meeting the needs of children with SEN;
- improving partnership approaches – inter-service collaboration in early years.

The period from age three to the end of the reception year (approximately 4.5 years of age) is now officially described as the

Foundation Stage, and represents an important phase in preparing children for later schooling and also for their personal social development. A set of early learning goals maps out what is expected for most children by the end of the Foundation Stage.

The importance of early years education in the context of SEN is that it offers opportunities for identification and assessment at an early stage in a child's life. Accepted best practice in SEN teaching indicates that early identification of a learning difficulty is a key to effective resolution. Not only do the requirements placed on early years settings ensure that the educational and social progress of children is systematically scrutinised at a young age, but also any **diagnosis** of SEN can immediately be acted upon with a greater likelihood of a successful outcome. All nursery and preschool settings are required to have a named person or **special educational needs coordinator** who assumes responsibility for SEN provision in their setting. Moreover, provision is subject to regular Ofsted (Office for Standards in Education, Children's Services and Skills) inspection, part of which is focused on the quality of arrangements to meet the identified SEN within the setting.

Discussion point/question: Why are some SEN more difficult to identify in the early years of schooling? What are the consequences of failing to recognise the difficulties being encountered by some children in their formative years?

Further reading

Wall, K. (2006) *Special Needs and the Early Years. A Practitioner's Guide.* London: Paul Chapman Educational Publishing.

See also: early intervention

EXCELLENCE IN CITIES

Before 1997 successive governments had failed to tackle the persistent problem of low attainment of schools in both urban and rural areas. The strong and pervasive link between poverty and underachievement had resulted in generations of **disadvantaged** pupils, many of whom were leaving school with no qualifications. Amongst these was an over-representation of children and young people with SEN. Earlier initiatives with a similar focus, in many ways the precursor of the Excellence in Cities initiative, had met with some success – for example, the 'educational priority areas' in the 1960s and the 'education action zones' of the 1990s. What was undoubtedly needed was a radical solution to an ongoing problem of educational underachievement. The Excellence in Cities programme was launched in 1999 with this end in view.

The Programme is a multi-strand initiative which attempts to address the failure of particular marginalised communities in both urban and rural settings. In doing so it operates across the age range of compulsory schooling. It has assimilated a large group of education action zones, now referred to as EiCAZs, of which there are 134. The Programme has established about 100 city learning centres, which provide sophisticated information and communication-based learning opportunities for the pupils at the host school, as well as for pupils in surrounding schools and for the community as a whole. Other initiatives include *Aimhigher*, designed to encourage marginalised groups to gain access to higher education, and the further development of learning support units (LSUs). The latter are school-based centres for pupils who are disaffected, at risk of **exclusion**, or vulnerable because of family or social issues. LSUs provide short-term teaching and support programmes tailored to the needs of pupils who need help in improving their behaviour, attendance or attitude to learning.

The Excellence in Cities programme is still ongoing. Indications are that there has been some impact in raising levels of achievement and aspirations, especially in connection with pupils experiencing certain SEN.

Discussion point/question: Try to find out some facts about 'education priority areas'. What similarities do you perceive between these and parts of the Excellence in Cities scheme?

Further reading

Machin, S., McNally, S. and Meghir, C. (2003) *Excellence in Cities: Evaluation of an Education Policy in Disadvantaged Areas*. Windsor: NFER.

See also: disadvantage; school effectiveness

EXTENDED SCHOOLS

An 'extended school' is one that provides a range of activities and services, often beyond the school day, 'to help meet the needs of its pupils, their families and the wider community' (DfES, 2005). One of the consistent linkages in SEN is that of the relationship between learning difficulties and social disadvantage. The latter has been summarised as the degree to which individuals within a community have access to certain facilities in order for them to maximise their potential as positive participants within that community. Such facilities include the provision of recreation and sport, health care, education and training, emotional support and welfare, and support and advice on relationships, employment and social well-being.

The idea of extended schooling had a recent roots impetus in the development of full-service schooling initiatives in the USA, which were frequently geared towards meeting the needs of 'at-risk' communities. The establishment of the community school initiative in Scotland (1999) was largely based on this approach.

The idea of centring the provision of different services on a single school site, or a cluster of schools, is not new, and there have been various examples of schools offering medical and welfare services alongside education since the middle of the nineteenth century. And in the 1960s and 1970s, the community schooling movement flourished in several urban (Coventry, Manchester, Birmingham) and rural (Leicestershire, Cambridgeshire) locations in England. The concept of 'community education' was a topic of significant scrutiny in educational literature.

In England, the beginnings of the contemporary version of community schooling are to be found in a Social Exclusion Unit report of 1998, which highlighted far lower pupil attainment in disadvantaged communities. In 2002, the (then) DfES began promoting the concept of the 'extended school'. It established schemes in 25 local authorities (LAs) to pilot extended schools. Each initiative was given a free hand to identify the focus of its work, though the emphasis was directed towards developing school provision which was characterised by such things as:

- facilities that are open to pupils, families and the wider community during and beyond the school day, before and after school hours, at weekends and during school holidays;
- providing activities aimed particularly at vulnerable groups, in areas of deprivation and/or where services are limited;
- having a positive effect on educational standards.

Many of the activities were targeted at pupils and were focused directly or indirectly on improving levels of learning. Understandably, one of the principal beneficiaries of this approach was likely to be the pupil with SEN, and especially those children from so-called 'marginalised' or 'isolated' families within communities.

More recently many LAs have been working towards a comprehensive provision of education, health and social care for children and families experiencing disadvantaging conditions. This has resulted in the designation of so-called 'full-service' schools in which all the necessary community services are located on a single school site.

Discussion point/question: How can SEN pupils benefit from what extended schools have to offer? How can such schools recognise whether their new role is having a positive impact?

Further reading

Cummings, C., Dyson, A. and Todd, L. (2004) *Evaluation of the Extended Schools Pathfinder Projects*. London: Department for Education and Skills.

See also: team around the child; disadvantage; professional collaboration

FAMILY THERAPY

The last twenty years has seen a significant growth, within education as a whole, of interest in the role of the family as part of a larger 'systemic' approach to supporting children's learning. Of course, there has always been a recognition that children learn best and become socially and emotionally well adjusted when they function as part of an established 'family'. This increased interest has come at a time when the composition of the traditional, nuclear family unit has changed and has come under increased pressure on account of social, cultural and moral shifts in society.

It is also important to recognise that, just as the function and position of the family in society has been subject to change, so too has the meaning of the word itself. It is now considered, therefore, that different cultures and different groupings often have very different notions of what 'family' means. One definition, which conveys the contemporary understanding of the term, is that from the Association of Family Therapists, which interprets 'family' as being any group of people who define themselves as such, and who care about and care for each other.

Moreover, it is regrettable to note that many SEN are linked with general disadvantage, and that social and economic disadvantage are implicated in a large number of cases of **emotional and behavioural difficulties**, family therapists help family members to explore different ways in which they can help each other. They work in non-judgemental ways, acknowledging 'real-life' contexts of families and respecting the different perspectives, beliefs, views and stories of each family member. In so doing, family therapists support both change in individuals and also in those involved in the various relationships that form part of the family. Their role, therefore, is to provide support to vulnerable families, who often include children with SEN amongst them.

Family therapy focuses on a diverse range of areas, and workers in this aspect of SEN support encounter circumstances which require skills in such things as child and adolescent mental health, emotional disorders including anxiety, depression and grief following bereavement.

Discussion point/question: What role can schools play when one of their SEN pupils is known to be involved in a family-therapy intervention?

Further reading

Barkley, R., Guevremont, D., Anastopoulos, A. and Fletcher, K. (1992) 'A comparison of three family therapy programs for treating family conflicts in adolescents with attention deficit hyperactivity disorder', *Journal of Consulting and Clinical Psychology*, 60(3) 450–62.

See also: disadvantage; nature and nurture; respite care

HOME TUITION

A requirement is placed on local authorities (LAs) to offer suitable education for pupils of compulsory school age who are otherwise out of school and/or not gaining qualifications (under Section 19, **Education Act 1996**). The term 'suitable education' is defined as that being appropriate to the age, ability and aptitude, and to any SEN the child or young person may have. Any decision regarding the nature of this provision has to be made in consultation with the child's parents, with the proviso that anything offered has to be consistent with the 'efficient' use of resources. Home tuition is a form of alternative provision. The term is a generic expression to cover both tuition supplied by an LA for children in their own home or by parents themselves in the home. In the case of the latter, a small number of parents decide to provide a suitable education for their child themselves. The law entitles them to do this (Section 7, Education Act 1996). Sometimes this is done in cases where a child is identified as having a 'school phobia' or when parents decide that their child is encountering emotional trauma because of bullying – both of which are linked to SEN.

Home tuition provided by the LA is often used when a pupil has been excluded from school as a result of unacceptable behaviour (**behaviour, emotional and social difficulties**) or where the pupil is awaiting placement in a special school or **pupil referral unit**. In such cases a qualified teacher, employed by the LA support services, will provide a structured programme of learning. This is planned in collaboration with the pupil's school and is linked to the existing targets that the pupil is working towards in an **individual education plan**.

Discussion point/question: Many pupils who are excluded from school are disaffected with learning. Why should home tuition make them more disposed to re-engaging with the formal curriculum?

Further reading

Elliott, J. (1999) 'Practitioner review: School refusal: Issues of conceptualisation, assessment, and treatment', *The Journal of Child Psychology and Psychiatry and Allied Disciplines*, 40, 1001–12.

See also: home–school relationship

HOSPITAL SCHOOLS

When children have a medical condition which requires their long-term hospitalisation, it is the responsibility of the hospital school to ensure that, dependent on the needs of individual children, they do not fall behind in school work. Not only does this enable the child's eventual return to school less stressful, but it also helps to 'normalise' their stay in hospital. Most large hospitals which have wards for children and young people have schools attached to them. They are staffed by qualified teachers and follow the **National Curriculum** as dictated by individual cases.

Hospital schools have a number of key aims. Foremost amongst these is to minimise the disruption to the child's formal education by providing continuity and offering effective teaching. In cases where a child has a long-term and complex medical condition which requires an extended stay in hospital, the intention is to provide a broad and balanced curriculum.

Staff in hospital schools need to be conscious of the fact that many children in hospital will encounter feelings of isolation, and they must therefore be aware of the need to minimise the emotional impact of these feelings. In addition, they have an important role in liaising with medical and nursing staff, and with teachers in the child's school.

Typically, lessons are taught both at the children's bedsides and in designated classrooms in the hospital or in small groups in areas set aside for this purpose.

Discussion point/question: What additional tensions and stressors do staff face when working with children who have serious long-term illness?

Further reading

Poursanidou, K., Garner, P., Stephenson, R. and Watson, A. (2003) 'Educational difficulties and support needs of children following renal transplantation: Student, parent and teacher perspectives', *International Journal of Adolescence and Youth*, 11, 157–80.

See also: support services; National Curriculum; differentiation

IDENTIFICATION AND ASSESSMENT

A key part of meeting the needs of children with SEN is the process of identification and assessment. Identification usually relates to an identification of a child's SEN, and leads to the assignment of a broad description of the child's learning difficulty. Assessment, whilst being an integral part of the identification process, is an ongoing process, as it is used over time to measure the progress that the child, once identified as having an SEN, is making in learning. Assessment therefore takes place at various stages in SEN provision and can be undertaken from a wide range of professional orientations – medical doctors, **educational psychologists**, **speech therapists** and so on. Some assessments, as in the case of those which lead to the provision of a **statement** of SEN, are multi-professional, and the recent introduction of the 'common assessment framework' (CAF) is further evidence of the interdisciplinary aspect of many assessments.

The SEN **Code of Practice** sets out clear arrangements for the process of assessment in schools and defines their responsibilities in connection with it. The emphasis on early identification has been a feature of effective SEN practice in schools over many years, and this is seen as one of the major features of best practice.

The initial responsibility for identifying SEN rests with the class teacher. Thus, for example, when a child starts primary school the class teacher, acting with the guidance of the school's **special educational needs coordinator** (SENCO), should begin the process of identification and assessment by using information arising from the child's previous educational experience to provide starting points for the development of an appropriate curriculum for the child. The **class teacher**, in this initial phase, should seek to identify the child's skills and strengths and try to build on these. At the same time the teacher would need to highlight areas for early action to support the child within the class. Typically this would be done by using curriculum assessment (i.e. how the child performs in reading or mathematics, for instance). This, and a process called 'baseline assessment', will allow the child to demonstrate what they know, understand and can do, as well as to identify any learning difficulties. During this process, a key to effective assessment of the child's needs will be regular and systematic observation by the teacher or **teaching assistant**.

As stated, the process of assessment is ongoing and is not solely conducted by teachers or SENCOs in school. Moreover, the move towards integrated services for children has placed a focus on the development of the CAF. This is an important strategy in ensuring that all work relating to children and young people is integrated and focused. The CAF is a standardised approach to conducting an assessment of a child's SEN and to deciding how those needs should be met; it is a framework which allows workers from different professional orientations and disciplines to contribute in an agreed and structured way to the assessment process. It is intended to provide a straightforward means of obtaining an holistic assessment of a child's SEN and (importantly) their strengths and aptitudes. Using the composite information obtained by this process, practitioners will be better placed to agree, with the child and family, about what further support is needed for the child.

Discussion point/question: Why is assessment such a vital element in curriculum provision for pupils who have SEN?

Further reading

Cline, T. (ed.) (1994) *The Assessment of Special Educational Needs – International Perspectives*. London: Routledge.

See also: early intervention; ability and attainment; normality and difference

INDIVIDUAL EDUCATION PLAN

An individual education plan (IEP) is an essential working document which enables teachers to plan, deliver and then evaluate a teaching intervention with a pupil who has a learning difficulty. It is a record of both the aptitudes and the needs of pupils as a means of establishing a baseline. This is used by teachers to set a series of targets (usually no more than three to four in each half term, which usually cover approximately six to seven weeks), as well as a set of indicators which allows progress towards meeting a target to be measured. A variant of the IEP is the 'group learning plan', in which targets are set for a small group of children who have similar or associated SEN.

An IEP also records how a particular teaching intervention should be managed. Thus an IEP will outline the personnel, resources and the teaching approach to be used and the timescale that will be needed to meet the identified learning targets. A termly review of the IEP will lead to the establishment of a revised version, which will be used to inform the next phase of learning and teaching.

Under the SEN **Code of Practice (2001)**, **class teachers** have a major role to play in the formulation and maintenance of the IEP. But the **special educational needs coordinator** has the ultimate operational responsibility for ensuring that the document is fit for purpose and that teachers and **teaching assistants** (TAs) in the school are using it correctly.

It is now accepted, as an indicator of best practice, that pupils and their parents are actively involved in the construction of the IEP. This includes their role in helping to set appropriate learning targets, as well as in periodic evaluation of its operation, and contributing to an annual review of the document. This level of participation is consistent with the contemporary emphasis on promoting the rights of all children and young people to have a say in their own education.

The notion of an 'IEP' does raise some interesting philosophical questions. In the first instance there has been a view expressed that individual learning programmes might not necessarily be consistent with the concept of **inclusion**. Thus, it is argued, pupils are not fully included in a classroom learning environment if they are working on separate programmes of study, and often with the ongoing input of a TA or other professional. This could, it is claimed, inhibit a pupil's full inclusion, especially in terms of social interaction with their peers.

A further issue relates to the contemporary trend of 'individualised' or 'personalised' learning. Whilst it could be argued that an IEP is a good manifestation of this approach, critics argue that if all learning is 'individualised' then all pupils in school, irrespective of their attainment levels or disability, should have an IEP.

IEPs were originally used in special schools, and have a much longer history of use in, for example, the USA. The Code of Practice (1994) was the first piece of statutory guidance to recommend that they should form a strategic part of the drive towards meeting SEN in mainstream settings. Initially there was a great deal of confusion regarding which pupils should be given an IEP, and who should construct it as well as its level of detail. The first 'phase' of IEP development, therefore, comprised a series of *ad hoc* attempts to respond to the 'guidance' provided in the Code of Practice. Many teachers claimed, with some justification, that the guidelines provided were far too loose and open to misinterpretation.

Discussion point/question: Why is it important that IEPs are seen as documents which all the key stakeholders – teachers, teaching assistants, parents, pupil and others – have direct input to?

Further reading

Tennant, G. (2007) 'IEPs in mainstream secondary schools: An agenda for research', *Support for Learning*, 22(4), 204–8.

See also: special needs coordinator; Code of Practice

INTENSIVE INTERACTION

Intensive interaction is a teaching approach used in instances where children and young people have severe learning difficulties relating to **communication** and **autism**, many of whom will still be in the earliest stages of developing communication. Intensive interaction focuses on teaching the pre-speech fundamentals for such children and young people.

Intensive interaction comprises a practical response to developing communication with children and young people with significant SEN. Its attractiveness is partly in that it does not require specialist equipment or facilities. The approach comprises a structured series of interaction sequences which emphasises relaxation and enjoyment. The interaction sequences are repeated frequently and gradually become more lengthy and complex sessions. During this time the teacher slowly introduces some of the fundamentals of communication, but does so by allowing the child or young person to determine the content and direction of the activity. Over time, with the teacher or other person always acting in a responsive and non-directive way, the child or young person becomes more familiar with an increasing range of ways of communicating, motivated by enjoyment. This way of working is based on the principles through which adults interact with babies in their early nurturing.

Discussion point/question: How can teachers and other persons be sure that the child who is the focus of intensive interaction is consenting to the intervention?

Further reading

Hewett, D. and Nind, M. (1998) (eds) *Interaction in Action: Reflections on the Use of Intensive Interaction*. London: David Fulton.

See also: autism; special schools

LEARNING STYLES

The notion that all people learn individually and according to a preferred learning style has become a major talking point in general education in the last ten or more years. A strong body of professional opinion suggests that attention to this is likely to bring big benefits for pupils with SEN, not least improvements in their academic achievement as well as increased levels of pro-social behaviour. The whole issue of learning styles has been widely publicised beyond formal education by the popularity of such things as Gardner's 'multiple intelligences' (Gardner, 1983). In SEN it has been the source of much discussion and development, especially with pupils who are underachieving in the curriculum.

The focus on learning styles has been reflected in the Primary National Strategy which contains an acknowledgement that attention to learning styles can be a major source of support for children's progress in school. There are many different theories of learning styles – different researchers have proposed different sets of learning characteristics. The concept is based on research which is indicating that individuals have a tendency to perceive and process information differently.

Many schools have examined a learning-style approach known as 'VAK', a classification based on different sensory perceptions – visual, auditory and kinaesthetic (VAK). This approach maintains that all children have a preferred (or dominant) learning style and that they will learn best if new ideas, skills and knowledge are presented in a way that appeals to this preference. This should not be taken to mean that pupils will always have a single or fixed way of learning. Indeed, most teachers who subscribe to 'learning-style theory' adopt a variety of learning styles.

In spite of such flexibility, the concept of learning styles has been challenged of late, with one commentator referring to it as 'educational snake oil'. So there is now a substantial debate regarding the value of interventions (not least in SEN) which emphasise the importance of learning styles. Indeed, a major government review was set up in 2004 to consider this in the context of further education. The study identified a number of criticisms of the learning-styles approach. These included the observation that there were frequent conflicts of interest in 'learning-styles research' because of the involvement of commercial organisations. The report argued that there were no clearly defined positive outcomes which could be linked to the application and practice of learning styles, and that much of the replication studies that had been undertaken were 'incestuous'.

Discussion point/question: What are your views about the differences in the way that various teachers have taught you in the past? Did you feel that you learned more effectively with one 'style' rather than another? What implications might this have for disaffected or struggling learners?

Further reading

Rayner, S. (2007) 'A teaching elixir, learning chimera or just fool's gold? Do learning styles matter?', *Support for Learning*, 22(1), 24–30.

See also: National Curriculum; differentiation

LIFE SKILLS

One of the most important elements of learning for all children whilst at school is referred to as 'life skills' or personal, social and health education. A life-skills programme provides pupils with opportunities to develop skills which allow them to become more independent and included members of society. This is done by providing pupils with a range of skills and insights to enable them to meet the demands of daily life, enabling them to take their place as citizens in their wider community.

Many children who experience learning difficulties have a relatively limited repertoire of social skills, and some find it difficult to make sense of, and interact with, the world around them. For such pupils, a training programme which provides them with information, skills and experiences designed for them to gain insights into everyday life, its opportunities, challenges and dangers, is both invaluable and necessary. Life skills are an integral element of **Every Child Matters**, in particular those elements of the strands relating to keeping safe and being healthy.

Discussion point/question: Should training in 'life skills' be part of the initial training of teachers?

Further reading

Norwich, B. and Kent, T. (2002) 'Assessing the personal and social development of pupils with special educational needs: Wider lessons for all', *Assessment in Education: Principles, Policy and Practice*, 9(1), 59–80.

See also: National Curriculum; school effectiveness

MAINSTREAM SCHOOLS

A mainstream school is one which caters for all pupils, including those with special educational needs. In some of the early literature on SEN relating to '**integration**', such schools have been referred to as 'ordinary schools', although this term is now regarded as somewhat unsatisfactory, as it conveys the notion of 'average' provision rather than that of excellence.

The term 'mainstreaming' has been very widely used in the USA and originating in the 1970s following the 1974 Individuals with Disabilities Education Act (IDEA), which was subsequently updated in 2004. This highlighted the importance of providing a 'least restrictive environment' for children with SEN, by stating that 'to the maximum extent appropriate, children with disabilities including children in public or private institutions or care facilities, are educated with children who are *non*-disabled; and special classes, separate schooling or other removal of children with disabilities from regular educational environment occurs only if the nature or severity of the disability is such that education in regular classes with the use of supplementary aids and services cannot be achieved satisfactorily'. (USA government, 2005).

Mainstreaming in education is the practice of bringing pupils out of the perceived isolation of special settings and into the 'mainstream' of educational life. In its earliest form, mainstreaming required that pupils with SEN should adjust as quickly as possible to the mainstream structures of the school. As with the concept of 'integration' in England, such an emphasis did little to ensure that schools themselves changed the way they functioned, so that the needs of the SEN pupil could be better met. The subsequent notion of '**inclusive education**', which emphasises the imperative for schools themselves to change the way they operate, has become a more widely held philosophy in both England and the USA, as it has elsewhere in the world.

In England the needs of pupils with SEN are currently met according to the requirements set out in the **Code of Practice** (2001). SEN is the responsibility of the whole school and is usually managed by the school's **special educational needs coordinator**. Provision is built around the twin strategies of **School Action** and **School Action Plus**. Most mainstream schools in England have developed good connections with **special schools** and settings, and some pupils are able to divide their timetable between the two schools, according to the needs that they have.

Discussion point/question: Is it viable for a single school to cater for the needs of every single child in a given location, irrespective of their learning needs or SEN?

Further reading

Norwich, B. (2006) 'Dilemmas in inclusive education', in R. Cigman (ed.) *Included or Excluded? The Challenge of the Mainstream for some Children with SEN*. London: Routledge.

See also: inclusion; special school

MULTI-SENSORY APPROACHES

Pupils with multi-sensory impairment have a combination of **visual** and hearing difficulties, which may be compounded by other disabilities too. They are still sometimes referred to as 'deaf-blind' but often may have some residual sight and/or hearing. Although many such pupils, as stated, have additional disabilities, the complexity of their various needs means that it can be difficult to determine precisely the nature of their intellectual abilities.

Understandably, pupils with multi-sensory impairments are faced with a far greater challenge in accessing the curriculum; indeed, they may be presented, in some schools, with the physical challenge of accessing the learning environment.

Children and young people who experience multi-sensory problems frequently have difficulties in perception, communication and in the acquisition of information. Both their incidental and inferential learning is limited: this means that they need much more direct teaching because they are unable to pick up the 'clues' that other learners utilise to help their learning to progress.

A complicating factor for them is that they can display high levels of anxiety, and experience profound levels of multi-sensory deprivation. These pupils need teaching approaches which make good use of their residual hearing and vision, together with their other senses. They may need alternative or augmentative means of communication.

In response to these needs, most special schools for children with severe, profound and complex needs now have purpose-built or adapted multi-sensory rooms, with music and light, and tactile and other soft-play resources to stimulate the children. The same facilities exist in a more limited number of mainstream schools. Many special schools also have hydrotherapy pools, providing an important opportunity for children to explore their own physical capabilities in a specialist environment.

Discussion point/question: How important is it that teachers and teaching assistants are familiar with how their SEN pupils seem to learn best? How can they discover this?

Further reading

Johnson, M. (2002) 'Multi-sensory teaching of reading in mainstream settings', in J. Wearmouth, J. Soler, and G. Reid, *Addressing Difficulties in*

Literacy Development: Responses at Family, School, Pupil and Teacher Levels. London: Routledge, 269–81.

See also: differentiation.

MUSIC THERAPY

Music therapy is widely used in many schools for children who have SEN. In straightforward terms it can be explained as having the potential to be both a diagnostic and a therapeutic intervention. It enables the therapist and/or others to arrive at an interpretation of a child's behaviour, whilst also providing opportunities for the child to communicate using a variety of musical forms. The aims of music therapy are primarily non-musical, and must obviously relate to the identified needs of each child. Thus, they may include the development of communication, and interaction skills, fostering an awareness of self and others, the growth of listening skills and the establishment of a supportive relationship.

Typically, therefore, the therapist will use the medium of music to engage a child in communication, allowing the child to take the lead in a 'conversation' which makes use of a variety of different sounds. This shared use of sound fosters a feeling of trust and engagement in the child, and consequently can allow the child to address issues which otherwise would remain dormant, with the danger that these might surface later on in life.

The use of music in a therapeutic mode has been documented with children and young people experiencing a diverse range of SEN. These include **autism, emotional and behavioural difficulties**, those with profound and multiple handicaps, and children and young people with speech, language and **communication** difficulties.

Moreover, there is also now considerable evidence of the use made of music in some schools and educational settings with general populations of children and young people. The evidence currently available suggests that it contributes positively to developing a 'climate for learning' as well as to the overall effective management of classrooms and whole schools. Because of this some educationists regard music therapy as an intervention that can be generically applied by teachers who are not formally trained as 'music therapists'.

Discussion point/question: As music is such a powerful and popular medium of expression for young people, should teachers make more use of it to encourage disaffected pupils to learn?

Further reading

Hallam, S. and Price, J. (1998) 'Can the use of background music improve the behaviour and academic performance of children with emotional and behavioural difficulties?', *British Journal of Special Education*, 25(2), 87–90.

See also: art therapy; drama therapy

NATIONAL CURRICULUM

The National Curriculum (NC) was introduced in 1988 as part of the **Education 'Reform' Act**. It represented the first time for almost 100 years that central government had sought to define the structure and content of the whole curriculum across all the years of compulsory schooling. It was immediately controversial, raising as it did big questions relating to equality of opportunity – and hence a substantive link to curricular provision for pupils with SEN. The proposals for the NC were especially controversial in respect of **assessment**, and there were fears expressed by teachers that what was being proposed was too prescriptive and target driven, and that there would be less opportunity to adapt the curriculum to meet the learning needs of pupils with SEN. Many of these concerns were subsequently shown to be largely unwarranted, especially as the NC as a whole was subjected to review and refinement in the succeeding 20 years.

The NC applies to all pupils of compulsory school age who are educated in community ('state'-funded) or voluntary schools. It is organised in four 'key stages'(KS): KS1, for pupils aged 5–7 years (Years 1 and 2 in primary school); KS2, for pupils aged 7–11 years (Years 3 to 6); KS3, for pupils aged 11–14 years (Years 7–9 in secondary school) and KS4, for pupils aged 14–16 years (Years 10–11).

But importantly, for SEN pupils the NC incorporated a statutory **inclusion** statement, which recognised that effective learning opportunities should be provided for all pupils, irrespective of their aptitudes or capabilities. Whilst the original working of the NC allowed for selective modification or 'disapplication', where a case could be made that a pupil would be incapable of coping, the NC enshrined three principles which were subsequently viewed as central to inclusive educational practice:

- setting suitable/appropriate learning challenges;

- responding to diverse learner needs;
- overcoming barriers to learning and assessment for individuals and groups of pupils.

The Education Act of 1988 (frequently referred to as the **Education 'Reform' Act**) emphasised the importance of access to the NC for *all* children. The original core NC documents all contained sections dealing with SEN, but these and the more recent replacements offered little real guidance for teachers, other than to urge **differentiation** of course materials or different rates of progress through key stages. However, the booklet entitled *Curriculum Guidance 2: A Curriculum for All* (NCC, 1989) does contain some useful advice. A similar publication, *Curriculum Guidance 9: The National Curriculum and Children with Severe Learning Difficulties* (NCC, 1992), attempts to promote access to the NC for children with severe disabilities. Since 1988 a burgeoning literature has developed concerning curriculum access, and especially differentiation. And it seems likely that this focus will prevail, as the focus on inclusion is sustained.

Recent years have seen the introduction of a number of initiatives to ensure that even pupils with the most complex and pronounced SEN have access to the NC, notably by way of the **performance scales**.

Discussion point/question: How important is it that pupils with SEN follow broadly the same curriculum as their peers? Is such an approach consistent with individualised learning?

Further reading

Lewis, A. (1996) 'Summative National Curriculum assessment of primary aged children with special needs', *British Journal of Special Education*, 23(1), 9–14.

See also: Education 'Reform' Act 1988

NATIONAL STRATEGIES (LITERACY AND NUMERACY)

Concerns regarding the standards achieved by children in literacy and numeracy have been consistently expressed by governments in England over many years, and continued even after the introduction of a national curriculum in 1988. One of the most visible policy responses to these concerns was the implementation of two National Strategies – in literacy and numeracy. The National Literacy Strategy was launched in 1997, with the National Numeracy Strategy following in 1998.

Whilst the strategies were generic in their orientation, there is little doubt that much of the thinking behind them was to address the challenge presented by those children who were underachieving in English and mathematics on account of a range of SEN. The strategies were focused on intervention work in the primary phase, and were built around an understanding that children who were struggling to read or to complete basic numeracy activities should be offered three levels of support, known as 'waves', which assumed a graduated response according to the level of difficulty in either literacy or numeracy being experienced by the child.

Wave 1 provided resources and support for teachers to effectively include all pupils, irrespective of the level they were learning at, in a high-quality 'literacy hour' and in a daily mathematics lesson. Wave 2 was characterised by small-group intervention, sometimes using specific reading or numeracy schemes which had been specifically developed for children who were seen to be struggling with the basic skills in these areas. Wave 2 interventions are not seen primarily as SEN interventions, although some of the pupils who are the focus of the interventions may be on **School Action** or **School Action Plus**.

Finally, in Wave 3, individual children would receive specific targeted support for pupils identified as requiring SEN support. This might comprise input from a speech therapist or the one-to-one support from a **teaching assistant** in following a particular reading scheme. All children at Wave 3 would be placed at School Action or School Action Plus.

Discussion point/question: Are any other aspects of the learning of pupils with SEN the subject of a nationally applied strategy? Why are literacy and numeracy initiatives so widely publicised?

Further reading

Berger, A., Henderson, J. and Morris, D. (1999) *Implementing the Literacy Hour for Children with Learning Difficulties*. London: David Fulton.

See also: school effectiveness; National Curriculum

NURTURE GROUP

Nurture groups have their origins in the 1970s when they were established to support those children who were unable to access the curriculum, either due to late development or an inability to regulate their behaviour. The theoretical underpinnings of nurture groups are based on the seminal work of Bowlby, who had developed a theory which, in general terms, regarded children's emotional health as being primarily based on the degree to which they are enabled to make effective relationships (in Bowlby's case the child's mother was central to this): it was referred to as 'attachment theory'. Nurture groups usually comprise children with a range of SEN (but generally those relating to social and emotional needs) who are taught in a separate classroom within the school. They are more common in primary schools, although the approach has started to be introduced into some secondary settings. Placement in a nurture setting is not permanent, with most children participating in this approach for no longer than three or four school terms. Moreover, they still remain a member of their class group for such generic school activities as registration, assemblies and a range of curriculum subjects.

Importantly, the use of nurture groups is a key element in supporting the mental health needs of children and can thus be linked to such recent initiatives as the **social and emotional aspects of learning** initiative. And it is obviously the case that, whilst nurture groups can be beneficial for diverse groups of pupils, they have been identified as being successful in providing support and enhancing the learning of those pupils with SEN. Research has highlighted their impact in raising the esteem and reducing unwanted challenging behaviour of pupils with special **emotional and behavioural difficulties**. Nurture groups are therefore important school strategies in supporting greater **inclusion**.

Discussion point/question: Why can providing children with a secure space and a series of focused interventions relating to their emotions benefit subsequent learning?

Further reading

Bennathan, M. (1997) 'Effective intervention in primary schools: What nurture groups achieve?', *Emotional and Behavioural Difficulties*, 2(3), 23–9.

See also: social and emotional aspects of learning

PAIRED READING

Paired reading is a structured approach to enable children to become more proficient readers. It can be used in a variety of situations, both with regard to children with SEN and with others. Paired reading can be used in preschool settings with children who are at a developmental stage of 'readiness to read'. Later it can be invoked to help those pupils who, having started to read, have been identified as lacking in confidence or the requisite skills necessary for the development of independent reading.

Paired reading is an approach which is structured and delivered over an extended period. It comprises supported or assisted reading and is based around texts which the pupil has had direct involvement in choosing. Books or other reading materials can either be fiction or non-fiction; they are above the independent readability level of the pupil being supported. In choosing reading materials, the primary concern is that it must be stimulating for the reluctant reader.

In one review of the effectiveness interventions for failing reading, paired reading ranked as one of the most effective (Brooks, Flanagan, Henkhuzens and Hutchison, 1998). It should however be noted that research into the effectiveness of the technique applies only to the explicitly structured technique of paired reading (as described by Topping, 2001).

The paired reading approach has been widely used, and it has been demonstrated to be effective with thousands of children. Unlike some reading interventions, follow-up studies suggest that the reading gains made are sustained and do not diminish with time. Furthermore, evidence points to increased levels of confidence and of greater social inclusion following programmes of **Reading Recovery**.

Discussion point/question: What difficulties might be encountered in setting up a home-based, paired-reading scheme? Would the obstacles be greater in some households than others? How might they be overcome?

Further reading

Topping, K.J. (2001) *Peer Assisted Learning: A Practical Guide for Teachers.* Cambridge, MA: Brookline Books.

See also: National Strategies; peer tutoring; Reading Recovery

PEER TUTORING

Peer tutoring involves helping pupils to support the learning of their peers. This can take many forms: sometimes older pupils can assist younger children. At other times pupils who are achieving at a higher level help children of the same age who may be struggling to learn. The concept of 'peer tutoring' is not a new one. In England, for instance, Bell and Lancaster used peer tutoring 200 years ago. Subsequently the approach has become popular in many locations worldwide. It is especially useful in supporting pupils experiencing SEN. Not only has peer-supported learning been shown to benefit SEN pupils by raising their attainment levels (Topping, 2001), but it is also an important strategy in promoting their more general social and educational inclusion.

Understandably, peer-tutoring approaches are closely associated with more specific paired-learning approaches, as in the case of **paired reading**. But a wide range of other subjects have also been the focus of this strategy, including mathematics, languages and science. And as in the case of paired reading, it is important to emphasise the learning gains of the pupil who is undertaking the role of the tutor. Moreover, research evidence suggests that peer tutoring also improves how both tutor and tutee feel about the subject area. They show more affinity with the subject and demonstrate greater confidence and better behaviour.

Peer tutoring is not a teaching approach which reduces teacher involvement in children's learning. To be successful it takes time and care to plan and implement. The pupils have to be carefully matched and appropriate material has to be selected. Both tutors and their tutees have also to be trained. And the teacher, **teaching assistant** or others need to carefully monitor the progress of both the tutor and the SEN pupil(s) in order to ensure that the intervention is having a positive impact. In spite of such time-consuming activity, peer tutoring is now recognised as a practice that classroom teachers can adopt to enable them to cater for an increasingly diverse range of SEN within an inclusive, mainstream classroom.

Discussion point/question: Why might children be more likely to learn from their peers?

Further reading

Topping, K.J. (2001) *Peer Assisted Learning: A Practical Guide for Teachers.* Cambridge, MA: Brookline Books.

See also: paired reading

PERFORMANCE INDICATORS ('P-SCALES')

One of the criticisms of the **National Curriculum** (NC)when it was first introduced in England in 1988 was that the assessment tasks which were formulated to measure pupil progress were not able to provide accurate or useful information regarding the curriculum progress of those pupils whose level of achievement fell below level 1 (on a 10-level range) of the NC performance levels. There were increasing concerns, expressed by practitioners, parents and policy makers, that it was impossible to assess whether interventions were being successful because they were independent of NC arrangements. As a result of these worries expressed especially by those working with pupils whose SEN were significant (for example, children with profound and multiple handicaps or severe learning difficulties), a set of Performance Indicators known as 'P-scales' was developed in 2001. These have become an important means of establishing baseline educational performance as well as target setting, and in establishing the 'value-added' benefits in teaching the most severely disabled pupils.

Discussion point/question: How important is it for teachers working with children with severe and complex SEN that they are able to assess the progress that the child is making? Who benefits most from P-scales?

Further reading

Martin, A. (2006) 'Assessment using the P scales: Best fit – fit for purpose?', *British Journal of Special Education*, 33(2), 68–75.

See also: National Curriculum; categories of SEN; inclusion and individual rights

PLAY THERAPY

Play therapy has been used over many years as a means of helping children to make sense of muddled feelings, upsetting or traumatic life events and the psychological impact of growing up in a complex and challenging contemporary world. As suggested, it is an approach in which children use play to communicate their feelings at their own level and at their own pace in a context which is non-threatening and has no sense that they are being subjected to 'interrogation'.

The use of 'play' in education has been the focus of considerable attention in the last ten years, and particularly so following the emergence of the **Every Child Matters** agenda. It is regarded as a core element of the **National Curriculum**'s 'Foundation Stage', although the recognition of the importance of play to a child's early development is by no means new. It is thus important to recognise that play is an important development strategy, and has a major role to play in enabling children to learn about the world around them.

The role of play in children's early development has been recognised since the time of Plato (429–347 BC). Plato observed that 'you can discover more about a person in an hour of play than in a year of conversation'. Subsequently such philosophers and educationists as Rousseau, Frobel and Montessori all emphasised its central importance in enabling adults to better understand the way that children think and act. Perhaps the first documented case of the therapeutic use of play was in 1909. In that year Freud first published his account of his work with 'Little Hans'. The latter was a five-year-old boy who had a phobia. Freud recommended that the boy's father should observe the way that Hans played, in order to provide insights that might assist the child.

Play therapy clearly has a role to play with children who are dealing with emotional turmoil and who may have been identified as experiencing **behavioural, emotional and social difficulties**. It enables them to receive emotional support and to learn to understand more about their own feelings and thoughts. Acting-out scenarios using play techniques help pupils to make sense of their past and cope better with their future, whilst also enabling them to manage relationships more effectively. Effective play-therapy intervention results in a reduction in anxiety, raised self-esteem and a greater capacity to participate in social situations. It is therefore an important strategy for the promotion of greater educational and social inclusion for some pupils with particular SEN.

Discussion point/question: Given the emphasis on the formal curriculum and sets of 'targets', do children have enough opportunities to engage in play in schools?

Further reading

Brodin, J. (2005) 'Diversity of aspects on play in children with profound multiple disabilities', *Early Child Development and Care*, 175, 635–46.

See also: early years education; drama therapy; art therapy

PROVISION MAPPING

Provision maps are a recent innovation, designed to provide an 'at a glance' way of documenting the range of support a school makes for children with SEN, additional staffing or peer support.

They are a form of SEN 'audit' tool which is useful to those with a leadership and management function (for example, **special educational needs coordinators** or head teachers) in respect of SEN. Provision maps tabulate the resources (teachers/**teaching assistants** and others) allocated to a given child with SEN, and the purpose of the resource allocation (in other words, what aspect of the child's SEN is being addressed by the intervention), together with the time and the likely financial cost of providing this support.

Provision maps can be used flexibly to record details of allocations of SEN support in a variety of ways. For instance, they can show the distribution of SEN resources according to the four areas of difficulty identified within the 2001 **Code of Practice** (**cognition and learning**; **communication and interaction**; **behaviour, emotional and social**; **sensory and/or physical**) or they can be used to compare provision at **School Action** and **School Action Plus**. Moreover, they are viewed by many as a proactive management tool which aids in forward planning, and as a means of ensuring that vital, but often scarce, resources are directed to appropriate areas of need within a school.

Discussion point/question: Do provision maps enable resources to be used more efficiently, or are they simply a further piece of bureaucracy for special educational needs coordinators to deal with?

Further reading

East Riding Council (2008) 'Provision mapping – An "at a glance" way of showing the range of provision', www.eriding.net/inclusion/provmap_res.shtml (accessed 16 July 2008).

See also: support services; team around the child

PUPIL REFERRAL UNIT

Pupil referral units (PRUs) have been established since 1996 as one of the ways in which local authorities can ensure that they can comply with the duty to provide suitable education for children of compulsory school age who cannot attend school.

A PRU is a small-scale educational setting, sometimes catering for less than 50 pupils. All will have some kind of SEN and many will have presented difficulties associated with behaviour. Some LAs use PRUs as a means of providing short-term interventions to address particular behaviours; this was, in fact, the way that PRUs were envisaged to operate when they were first established. PRUs also provide education for a range of other learners, including those who are unable to attend school because of medical problems, pupils who have been assessed as being school phobic and pregnant schoolgirls.

The forerunner of the PRU originated in the late 1960s and early 1970s. This was the so-called 'disruptive unit' (sometimes coyly entitled a 'study centre'). These were established by LAs in many locations in England to deal exclusively with pupils (predominantly boys) whose behaviour was becoming increasingly unmanageable in **mainstream schools**. The majority of units at that time dealt with the behavioural needs of secondary-aged pupils. During the 1980s a number of highly critical reports were published, particularly highlighting the lack of educational progress being made by the pupils and the poor subject knowledge and pedagogy of the teachers. Moreover, these critical reports suggested that once a pupil was placed in a 'unit' it was unlikely that they would return to their mainstream school.

Contemporary PRUs cater for particular kinds of pupil (those with emotional as opposed to behavioural difficulties, for example, as well as those dedicated units for teenage mothers). As with their predecessors, PRUs mainly cater for boys who present behaviour difficulties. The most obvious difference between the two is the extent to which contemporary PRUs now follow a more systematic curriculum, closely aligned to mainstream provision. Moreover, the educational and social progress of the pupils in PRUs is now far more closely scrutinised than previously, and there is evidence that many pupils in such settings are achieving at a higher level than was the case in the earlier version of off-site provision.

One of the key characteristics of provision by a PRU is its flexibility. It can provide both full-time and part-time education for pupils. There is now a far more strategic view taken regarding reintegration back into mainstream settings than was previously the case, and PRU staff work in a collaborative way with both teachers in mainstream schools and other support agencies. They frequently have good links with local vocational training opportunities, including further education colleges.

Discussion point/question: Why do some PRUs find it difficult to reintegrate pupils to their mainstream settings?

Further reading

Garner, P. (1996) 'A la recherche du temps PRU', *Children and Society*, 10(3), 187–96.

See also: disruptive behaviour; emotional and behavioural difficulties; inclusion

READING RECOVERY

Reading Recovery was developed in the 1970s by New Zealand educator Dr Marie Clay, and is now a well-established scheme for supporting children with SEN in reading difficulties. Clay, after observing the way in which successful early readers developed, defined reading as a message-getting, problem-solving activity, and developed 'Reading Recovery' as a strategy to address children's difficulties in this area. It stresses the development of phonological awareness and the use of contextual information to assist in reading development. Clay and other advocates of this approach maintain that it is an educationally sound and cost-effective early intervention which helps children who are struggling to read during the early years of their primary schooling..

The emphasis in Reading Recovery is very much on a structured programme which is planned as an extended set (between 12 and 16 weeks) of daily half-hour sessions with specially trained Reading Recovery teachers. It is directed mainly towards six-year olds in the bottom 20 per cent of their class in terms of their reading achievement. Typically, lessons comprise reading books, letter identification, word 'making-and-breaking' exercises and story writing.

Many local authorities in England have adopted Reading Recovery, and evaluations of its success have shown that children participating in the programme have made significantly greater progress than children who received alternative intervention strategies. The approach has been adopted by a major national charity, Every

Child a Reader, which is sponsoring Reading Recovery programmes for nearly 40,000 children a year in inner-city schools around the UK. There are 600 trained Reading Recovery teachers.

Discussion point/question: As there are now several adults, apart from the teacher, in most primary classrooms, will this stimulate further developments in Reading Recovery?

Further reading

Schwartz, R. (2005). 'Literacy learning of at-risk first grade students in the Reading Recovery early intervention', *Journal of Educational Psychology*, 97, 257–67.

See also: National Curriculum; National Strategies (Literacy and Numeracy); cognition and learning

RESIDENTIAL SPECIAL EDUCATION

Residential schools for children and young people with more severe or complex needs have been commonplace in the English education system for many years. Historically those with significant disabilities or mental handicap were isolated from mainstream society in 'asylums' or other institutions. These were traditionally located in isolated settings, away from centres of population, and those who occupied them became, over time, the object of both suspicion and pity. Little was provided in the way of education; the emphasis was on care and welfare. Charitable benefactors from the new industrial middle classes, social reformers and, subsequently, charitable organisations were mainly responsible for this early provision.

Latterly, in the mid-twentieth century, residential schools providing education and training were established in many parts of England. These catered for children with diverse learning difficulties, but most frequently these were severe and complex, and physical, medical and psychological in nature. Almost all these children will hold a statutory **'statement'** of SEN, issued by their local authority (LA). Three main types of residential provision remain in existence in England at the present time:

- 'State' or 'maintained' schools funded entirely by the LA. Such schools have decreased significantly in number, mainly as a result of the dramatic increase in the cost of providing 24-hour care and educational provision, but also because of the increased emphasis on the right of individual children to be educated in mainstream settings.

- 'Non-maintained' schools run by charitable trusts. These charge fees, predominantly to ensure that the school remains financially viable.
- 'Independent' schools. These are wholly funded by fees and often run on a profit-making basis.

All residential provision for children with SEN has to be approved by the Department for Children, Schools and Families. Moreover, they are subject to periodic inspection by the Office for Standards in Education, Children's Services and Skills (Ofsted) and by the Commission for Social Care Inspection, which inspects care standards in residential schools and in children's homes.

Although 'state' residential schools are required to follow the **National Curriculum** (albeit in an adapted format, appropriate to the needs of the children concerned), other forms of residential provision are not. In spite of this, they frequently choose to organise their curricular provision so that it is consistent with the main features of the National Curriculum, thus contributing to a smoother transition between the residential experiences they offer and that of **mainstream** and other settings.

Discussion point/question: Residential schools for children with SEN have been criticised as being more like nineteenth-century asylums. Is such an extreme view fair? What are the positive benefits they bring to children with SEN?

Further reading

Morris, J., Abbott, D. and Ward, L. (2003) 'Disabled children and residential schools: The implications for local authority professionals', *British Journal of Special Education*, 20(2), 70–5.

See also: special schools and settings; inclusion

RESPITE CARE

Some children who have profound or severe SEN require intensive round-the-clock care, either because of their medical needs or because their SEN is such that it means that they are at risk of injury or harm if they are unsupervised. 'Respite care' is the provision of short-term, temporary relief to those who are caring for family members who might otherwise require permanent placement in residential school or other settings outside the home. Although most families are very committed to caring for children with significant SEN, the process of providing long-term care can be hugely demanding. The physical and emotional impact on individual family members can be substantial, and can result in deterioration in the quality of care that is provided. Respite care comprises the provision, usually by government or by voluntary organisations and charities, of a much needed temporary break from the often exhausting challenge of undertaking a full-time care role by family members.

Provision of respite care has been shown to be a positive way of supporting families. It helps to sustain the health and well-being of family care givers, reduces substantially the likelihood of abuse and neglect of SEN children within families, and helps maintain other family relationships. In spite of these positive outcomes, respite care is often very difficult for families to access, partly on account of the increasingly high cost of the specialised care needed for children with severe and complex SEN.

Discussion point/question: Should there be a more systematic way of ensuring that all families which include a child or young person with severe and complex needs receive an entitlement to respite care?

Further reading

Chadwick, O., Beecham, J., Piroth, N., Bernard, S. and Taylor, E. (2002) 'Respite care for children with severe intellectual disability and their families: Who needs it? Who receives it?', *Child and Adolescent Mental Health*, 7(2), 66–72.

See also: team around the child; support services

SANCTIONS AND REWARDS

Teaching interventions with pupils who present behaviours which are deemed appropriate (described elsewhere in this book as forming part of the SEN term now most commonly associated with this learning difficulty – behavioural, emotional and social difficulty) have long used a balance between rewards and sanctions. The latter has historically been referred to as 'punishment', although the current emphasis in managing pupil behaviour is on the use of rewards to prompt positive behaviour. It is obviously important to bear in mind that the use of rewards and sanctions applies to all pupils, irrespective of the nature of their learning.

There is widespread agreement amongst most educationists that rewards are more effective than punishment in motivating pupils. If a teacher uses frequent praise and rewards positive behaviour, pupils will be encouraged to adopt pro-social behaviours. As a result, most 'behaviour training' emphasises that teachers need to try to highlight such behaviours, and give positive feedback to the pupil when it occurs. One of the most influential reports on discipline in schools, by Lord Elton (1989), noted that a rewards:sanctions ratio of at least 5:1 ought to be aimed for. Similarly, the more recent *Learning Behaviour* report (2005) recommended that a wide range of rewards and sanctions are applied fairly and consistently.

Rewarding positive behaviour is based on the basic psychological theory of reinforcement, which in turn leads to greater motivation and learner confidence. Of course, rewards can take many forms, and most schools have a consistent, whole-school view on what is appropriate in a given situation. One of the most obvious forms of reward is the use of 'teacher praise'. This is of especial importance to pupils with SEN in that research has suggested that these children are least likely to be the recipients of positive comments from a teacher. Praise can comprise the frequent use of encouraging language, gestures and eye contact. Most schools also have a formal system of credits, merits and prizes to give recognition to pupils when they set a good example, demonstrate effort and commitment, or show improvement in their behaviour.

Discussion point/question: Reflecting on your own time in school, which rewards and sanctions were the most effective? Which were the least effective? Why do you think this was the case?

Further reading

Moberly, D., Waddle, J. and Duff, R. (2005) 'The use of rewards and punishment in early childhood classrooms', *Journal of Early Childhood Teacher Education*, 25(4), 359–66.

See also: behaviour for learning; disruptive behaviour; social and emotional aspects of learning

SCHOOL ACTION AND SCHOOL ACTION PLUS

New within-school arrangements for ensuring that the needs of children are met were introduced by the 2001 **Code of Practice**. These were built around a graduated arrangement of provision, and comprised two stages, referred to as School Action and School Action Plus. Both have become an integral element of the school-based procedure for meeting SEN.

In cases where a child does not progress in their learning, and fails to respond to differentiated teaching approaches, there is a need for the school to attempt something that is either additional or different. This type of provision is described in the Code of Practice as 'school action'. In **early years education** a similar arrangement obtains, this being described as 'early years action'.

School Action comprises a range of different initiatives, dependent on the difficulties experienced by the SEN child. This could involve a new approach to teaching the child, the use of different teaching materials and it might involve the use of additional adult support. The whole process of School Action intervention is recorded in the child's **individual education plan**.

In cases where the child has failed to progress in spite of the various inputs at the School Action stage, the school will respond by invoking the School Action Plus element in its graduated provision. At this stage the school seeks external advice from various local-authority support services, or from health or social work professionals. This advice will vary, according to the needs of the child. It may, for example, include inputs from a speech and language therapist or a behaviour support specialist. These professionals will offer advice and support to school staff in their work with the child. In some cases there will be an agreement regarding additional resources.

In most cases children and young people with SEN will have their needs met at either the School Action or School Action Plus stage. But if a child's needs cannot be met through School Action Plus, the local authority, in conjunction with the school and the parents, may consider the need for a statutory assessment, possibly leading to a **statement** of SEN.

Discussion point/question: What types of evidence do you think that a special needs coordinator would need to assemble for a child to move from School Action to School Action Plus? Why is it so important for this evidence to be available?

Further reading

Cowne, E. (2008) *The SENCO Handbook. Working within a Whole-School Approach.* London: Routledge.

See also: Code of Practice

SOCIAL AND EMOTIONAL ASPECTS OF LEARNING

The social and emotional aspects of learning (SEAL) relate to those qualities and skills that enable children to manage life and learning effectively. There has always been a focus on what might be termed the 'affective' (as opposed to cognitive) aspects of learning, and recent years have seen a dramatic increase in awareness by educationists of its importance. This has in part been fuelled by the widespread publicity given to related work in this field. Gardner (1983), for example, highlighted the notion of 'multiple intelligences', including being intelligent about our own emotions (intrapersonal intelligence) and about those of others (interpersonal intelligence). Similarly, Goleman (1996) used the expression 'emotional intelligence' and pointed out that emotional and social skills are perhaps more influential than conventional interpretations of intelligence for effective personal and career development. The rise in concern about children's antisocial behaviour, together with a widespread concern about the mental health of young people, led to a concerted effort by central government to develop viable programmes to assimilate this thinking for the purpose of providing support and guidance to children and young people. Whilst the subsequent SEAL initiatives were directed towards the generic school population, the programmes have a particular relevance to those children and young people who are 'at risk' of school failure, often because of a range of SEN.

SEAL programmes now operate at both primary and secondary levels of schooling. Both are based on the same five social and emotional aspects of learning: self-awareness, managing feelings, motivation, empathy and social skills. These are regarded as the underlying qualities which relate to every aspect of a child's (and an adult's) life. Being aware and proficient in the skills that are subsumed within each of these five qualities enables children to be more effective learners, and to be able to get on with other children, and begins the process of preparing them to be responsible citizens.

Both primary and secondary SEAL initiatives are supported by extensive resources, which teachers can use flexibly in class (either in dedicated SEAL or in personal, social and health education or embedded within their **National Curriculum** teaching), or in school assemblies or other activities. There is also a substantial range of teacher resources to provide training and professional development in SEAL-related activities.

Some children who experience learning difficulties encounter problems of social isolation, communication difficulties, and a lack of self-esteem and confidence, as well as sometimes finding it difficult to avoid conflict situations and arguments. The SEAL programme attempts to address these issues in a structured way, and is therefore of considerable importance as a support mechanism for SEN pupils.

Discussion point/question: In what ways can being 'emotionally literate' assist in the development of the learning of children who have SEN?

Further reading

Ripley, K. (2006) *First Steps to Emotional Literacy*. London: David Fulton.

See also: mental health

SPECIAL SCHOOLS AND SETTINGS

Special schools are separate settings which have been established for children and young people who (usually) have a statutory **statement** of SEN. They can either be maintained by a local authority, or be an independent institution established by a charity, individual benefactor or, as is increasingly the case, commercial 'not-for-profit' organisations. Traditionally, special schools will cater for the educational needs of pupils who experience significant levels of learning difficulty and disability, and who require specialist intervention strategies to address their needs.

Special schools provide individualised education for children who experience the full range of learning difficulties: physical disabilities, including **visual** and hearing impairments, severe and profound learning difficulties, and **emotional and behavioural difficulties**. Because of the high level of educational need, the pupil:teacher ratio is normally low (typically between 6:1 and 10:11, depending on the level of need). Moreover, teachers working in such schools are supported by specialist **teaching assistants**, as well as an array of other professionals, some of whom are permanently attached to the school. These schools will also have special facilities, such as soft-play areas, sensory rooms, hydrotherapy pools and so on. Individual teaching spaces are usually equipped with specialist resources and are designed in ways that enable access and movement. Essential equipment like hoists, electronic aids and switches are provided to support learning, as well as design features to enable pupils to maximise the benefits of being in a specialist environment.

Since the **Education Act 1981** the role of special schools has been the subject of considerable debate. This has increased in intensity, and has become polarised. Advocates of 'full **inclusion**' maintain that special schools represent a denial of the right of SEN pupils to participate in 'full society', and as such they are an anachronism at a time when the **United Nations Convention on the Rights of the Child (1989)** is regarded as the hallmark of international agreement on how children and young people should be protected. Thus, the Convention states that all children have a right 'to express an opinion and to have that opinion taken into account, in any matter or procedure affecting the child' (Article 12), and that 'special care, education, health care, training, rehabilitation, employment preparation and recreation ... shall be designed in a manner conducive to the child achieving the fullest possible social integration and individual development, including his or her cultural and spiritual development.' (Article 23).

A contrary view is presented by those who regard the quest for 'full inclusion' as a dogma which cannot be applied to all pupils, and that there will be some who, because of their particular needs, will be best educated in specialist school environments. Moreover, these advocates suggest that the drive towards inclusion is led by financial, rather than moral or ethical concerns: special schools are far more costly to run than **mainstream settings**.

At the present time approximately 2.5 per cent of the school-age population is being educated in special schools. Parents still have the right to choose which school will most fit the needs of their child and many express a preference for separate special schooling.

More recently, too, there has been an emphasis on the need to view inclusive practice as one which comprises a flexible continuum of provision. This orientation is based on a view that special schools assist in the process of **inclusion** because in many cases they provide pupils with sets of vocational and life skills which enable them to secure a place in the wider community when they finally move from school into employment or training. Proponents of this viewpoint believe that rather than interpreting 'inclusion' as a concept defined by 'place', it is far more productive to view it as an open-ended concept which has as much relevance to special schools as it does to mainstream settings.

Discussion point/question: Can special schools and settings provide children and young people with skills and experiences that they would not be able to gain from attending mainstream settings?

Further reading

Jenkinson, J.C. (1996) *Mainstream or Special? Educating Students with Disabilities*. London: Routledge.

See also: integration; inclusion; mainstream schools

STATEMENT OF SEN

A statement of SEN sets out a child's needs and indicates the resources, support and specialist equipment which will enable those needs to be met. The statement is reviewed annually to ensure that the support provided is effective in meeting the child's needs. The statement is a legally binding document. For those children with profound, severe and complex needs it is likely that, even prior to beginning school, their needs will have been identified and they will already have had considerable specialist provision in the first few years of their life; such children will receive a statement of SEN as soon as they enter formal schooling. The process of acquiring an SEN statement for children whose learning difficulties are identified after starting formal education is set in motion if a child does not progress according to expectations as set out at the **School Action** and **School Action Plus** stages.

The statement of SEN sets out in detail the SEN of the child and provides a similarly detailed account of the additional support that the child will receive to address their difficulties. The first stage in establishing a statement of SEN entails a statutory, multidisciplinary **assessment**. If there is a consensus that a *prima facie* case has been made, a statement of SEN will be issued.

The statement of SEN comprises six parts:

- Part 1 provides substantive information on the child (name, address, date of birth).
- Part 2 describes the child's SEN, together with their strengths and aptitudes. This will be based on records of assessments, reports and observations undertaken previously by those professionals who have been involved with the child. This includes the child's **class teacher** and input from the parent/carer.
- Part 3 gives information concerning what additional support the local authority (LA) believes the child requires in order to meet the needs listed in Part 2. It also sets out the long-term aims of the statement in relation to the child's needs. Finally, this part of the statement gives information on how this work will be recorded and monitored.
- Part 4 relates to the choice of school which the child will attend. Parents have a legal right to express a preference in this regard – whether this be a **mainstream** or **special school** or setting. In cases of disagreement, specific resolution procedures (the **SEN Tribunal**) can be called upon to arbitrate.
- Parts 5 and 6 describe any other (non-educational needs) the child has and for which support will be required, and the details on how these needs will be met by (for example) health-care services.

The number of children and young people with statements of SEN in England was 236,500 in 2007. Of these children, around 57 per cent were placed in maintained mainstream schools or units and special classes in maintained mainstream schools. The numbers of children who have a statement of SEN has remained fairly constant over the years.

The granting of a statement, because it carries with it a requirement to resource all the actions and interventions within it, remains a complex process, in spite of recent changes to ensure that the process is completed within a specific time frame. And it also brings significant tensions, not least because LAs, who are required to provide the financial resources to ensure that appropriate provision is made, have limited funds and seek to ensure that these are used across a range of needs: individual statements are costly to maintain. As a result, there are sometimes conflicts between parents and the LA, which are often only resolved by an SEN Tribunal.

Discussion point/question: Should the acquisition of a statement of SEN be based (even in part) on the LA's capacity to pay for it? Or are statements of SEN an entitlement, irrespective of cost?

Further reading

Florian, L. (2002) 'The more things change the more they stay the same? A response to the Audit Commission's report on statutory assessment and statements of SEN', *British Journal of Special Education*, 29(4), 164–9.

See also: Education Act 1981

SUPPORT SERVICES

In meeting SEN in their location, local authorities (LAs) are required by the **Education Act 1996** to provide a range of support services to maintained (though not independent) schools. The term 'support services' in this context refers to all the human and material resources which support children and young people who have SEN. This includes such things as the provision of specialist support, materials and other resources. Some services which have traditionally been supplied to schools by LAs are now directly bought in by schools as a result of the greater devolvement of central LA funds to individual schools. The rationale behind this approach is that it provides schools with greater choice and flexibility in selecting the services that they require. One service which currently remains exempt from such delegation is the educational psychology service.

A key characteristic in the working arrangements of support services has been the development of multi-professional teams in many LAs. These cover a range of SEN-related services, including a behaviour support service, a service for looked-after children (children in the care of the LA), and that dealing with the social **inclusion** of pupils. This way of working, which has gradually emerged during the period following the **Education Act 1981**, has provided a sound basis for the more recent and rapid development of integrated local services delivery and good inter-agency links. This is well illustrated by the development of overarching **children's services** in LAs in England, which incorporate all support agencies to ensure a more 'joined-up' approach. SEN support services also provide support and advice to parents and professionals concerning the full range of SEN.

Discussion point/question: What are the advantages of effective joint working in support of SEN pupils? Do you perceive any potential tensions?

Further reading

Blamires, M. and Moore, J. (2006) *Support Services and Mainstream Schools: A Guide for Working Together*. London: Routledge.

See also: children's services; professional collaboration

SUPPORT TEACHING

When children have learning difficulties they present additional challenges to teachers. An already complex task of planning, delivering and evaluating a lesson becomes an even more difficult activity: amongst the 25 or so pupils will be some who have a variety of SEN, adding a further considerable challenge to the teacher's professional skills.

The increased diversity of learners in classrooms, and the nature of the task facing teachers, has been recognised by educational policy makers, especially in the period since the **Education Act 1981**. The need to provide support to teachers in the classroom became even more apparent as education provision began to be incorporated into integrated 'services for children' (now referred to as **children's services**). As these became prominent features of the educational landscape with the advent of the **Children Act 1989**, the role of 'support teaching' was consolidated and became a designated professional group – that of the **teaching assistant** (later to be extended to incorporate the 'higher-level teaching assistant'). The role of the teaching assistant is to provide support to the **class teacher** in a variety of capacities. These are described under a separate entry.

Discussion point/question: Does having 'additional adult help' in a classroom automatically benefit children with SEN? How can schools best ensure that this extra support is made best use of?

Further reading

Howes, A. (2003) 'Teaching reforms and the impact of paid adult support on participation and learning in mainstream schools', *Support for Learning*, 18 (4), 147–53.

See also: teaching assistant

TEAM AROUND THE CHILD

The 'team around the child' (TAC) is a model of service provision in which a variety of stakeholders from a range of different professions come together to provide help and support in relation to the SEN of an individual child. The ethos of the TAC approach is that the emphasis is placed firmly on the real needs of the child, rather than on what is convenient or cost-effective to professionals and service providers.

The TAC approach is flexible. It does not imply a multidisciplinary team that works together all the time, or is located in a single building or office. On the contrary, this grouping comes together as required, thus making the most effective use of what are increasingly costly specialist resources. This flexible way of working is a crucial feature of the way that **children's services** function, and it enables the team to meet a diverse range of SEN. Importantly, parents and carers are centrally involved as part of the team.

Discussion point/question: Is the concept of the 'team around the child' just another piece of SEN jargon, coining a catchy phrase to describe the collaborative provision that has been emerging over a number of years?

Further reading

Siraj-Blatchford, I., Clarke, K. and Needham, M. (eds) (2007) *The Team Around the Child: Multi-Agency Working in the Early Years.* Stoke-on-Trent: Trentham Books.

See also: support services; professional collaboration; parent partnership

WHOLE-SCHOOL SEN POLICY

The concept of a whole-school policy has become a central feature in both policy and administration in schools over the last 25 years or so. Whole-school policies can relate to a wide range of educational issues – bullying, **assessment**, discipline and equal opportunities are examples. The current statutory guidance on SEN in schools (the **Code of Practice** (2001)) requires that all schools develop and sustain a common approach to SEN provision. Most schools do this in the form of a whole-school SEN policy.

The Code of Practice sets out guidance on what an SEN policy should contain. Maintained schools must publish information about their SEN policy in the governing body's annual report. This must describe principles on allocating resources among SEN pupils, and should be accessible to the whole school community – including parents.

The Code gives advice on what a whole-school SEN policy should contain. Generally speaking, school policies should show how the school's overall objectives and mission statement address the needs of children with learning difficulties. This is sometimes included in an '**inclusion** statement'.

The whole-school policy provides information regarding who has strategic responsibility for SEN in the school – for instance, it must include the name of the person responsible for coordinating day-to-day provision for SEN (this is normally the **special educational needs coordinator**). It must also specify the roles and responsibilities of other teachers, and those of the head teacher and the school's **SEN governor**.

The SEN policy will also map out the day-to-day operation of the school's SEN policy, and in doing so provide details of such things as liaising with teachers and **teaching assistants**, record keeping, relationships with parents and with supporting professionals, and professional development arrangements in SEN. Finally, the school is required to keep its SEN policy under regular review.

Discussion point/question: Why is it so vital that a school has an SEN policy which is subscribed to by all those who work there?

Further reading

Tarr, J. and Thomas, G. (1997) 'The quality of special educational needs policies: time for review?', *Support for Learning*, 12(1), 10–14.

See also: social and emotional aspects of learning; class teacher; school effectiveness

PUPILS, PROFESSIONALS AND PARENTS

CHILD AND ADOLESCENT MENTAL HEALTH SERVICES

An important aspect of the **Every Child Matters** agenda was the focus on the health and well-being of children. This issue has been a matter of growing concern in England, as many children and young people have shown evidence of experiencing mental-health problems. Explanations for this are varied, ranging from the negative impact of a rapidly changing society, pressure from peers and from the media, and emotional trauma as a result of the unrealistic expectations placed on them by schools and society as a whole. An illustration of the extent of the problem is provided by data obtained in a study from 2000, which suggested that 10 per cent of the school-aged population suffered from mental-health issues, with boys being more liable to experience difficulties than girls.

Child and adolescent mental-health services (CAMHS) were established partly in response to these concerns and partly because there were widespread discrepancies in the provision for children who had SEN relating to mental-health issues. In 1995, the NHS Health Advisory Service proposed a four-tier model for providing a comprehensive service of mental-health provision, an approach which was later applied by the Audit Commission and recognised by government in its funding plans for CAMHS in 1999. CAMHS are now an established aspect of provision, and, in the context of SEN, primarily address issues relating to **emotional and behavioural difficulties** (EBD). They comprise multidisciplinary mental-health services which offer assessment, treatment and support for children and young people and their families.

The term 'child and adolescent mental-health service' is used to describe two different ways of operating. It is most commonly used as describing the overarching provision available from those services that contribute to the mental-health care of children and young people. This includes services provided by health, education, social services and other agencies. Used in this way, the term also includes generic services which, whilst not having a primary focus on health care, will nevertheless have significant contact with it as a result of dealing with the additional needs of some pupils with SEN. The term is occasionally used in a more specific way, in reference to specialist child and adolescent mental-health services, often working in a clinical context with more severe cases of mental illness.

CAMHS operate according to 'tiers' of provision, with Tier 1 and Tier 2 being the most common levels in which schools will be involved. At Tier 1 general advice and support is offered in cases which are less complex or extreme. Typically this might involve a CAMHS worker being involved with teachers in helping them to address particular EBD issues with a pupil or small group of children; or they may offer advice regarding the promotion of mental-health issues in a school context. At Tier 2 the provision is more directed towards working with specific cases; for example, primary mental-health workers, psychologists and counsellors might work in a school, doctors' surgery or health centre, offering consultations to a teacher, doctor or a family in connection with more serious mental-health needs.

Discussion point/question: Why have the mental-health needs of children and young people tended to be less high profile than other SEN?

Further reading

Carpenter, B. and Morgan, H. (2003) 'Count us in: The role of schools and colleges in meeting the mental-health needs of young people with learning disabilities', *British Journal of Special Education*, 30(4), 202–5.

See also: normality and difference; emotional and behavioural difficulties; social and emotional aspects of learning

CLASS TEACHER

Under the 1994 and 2001 **Code of Practice**, **class teachers** have been given significant responsibility for meeting the needs of children with SEN in their classes. The Code states that they must make the first **assessment** of the learning level of the child, in order to determine whether there are signs of underachievement. Thus, if a child has an identified SEN when they start school, the child's class teacher should, in consultation with the head and the **special educational needs coordinator** (SENCO), use information arising from the child's previous educational experience to provide starting points for the development of an appropriate curriculum. The class teacher has to establish what the child's educational capabilities are via what is referred to as a 'baseline assessment'. This shows the teacher what the child can do, as well as the areas in which he or she is having difficulty. Once these are identified, the class teacher then has to introduce learning strategies designed to address the learning difficulties presented by the pupil. The class teacher also has to ensure that, once learning gets under way, the process is kept under review, and that regular liaison takes place between the SENCO, other teachers and **teaching assistants**, and especially parents. Liaison with the latter is particularly important, and forms one of the cornerstones of educational legislation in the last 20 years as it is a core element of ensuring that the child's rights are protected. The class teacher must also use the evidence from their regular assessments to help them plan the next stage of the child's learning. Crucially, the **Code of Practice** refers to the class teacher's involvement in the production and development of **individual education plans** (IEPs), which are introduced in cases where the initial intervention plan appears to have little or no effect in improving the child's level of achievement. The class teacher needs to interact very closely with the SENCO in order to formulate and then maintain the IEP.

Discussion point/question: What kind of initial training does a teacher receive for them to be able to take the initial responsibility for SEN in their classroom?

Further reading

Fox, S., Farrell, P. and Davis, P. (2004) 'Factors associated with the effective inclusion of primary-aged pupils with Down's syndrome', *British Journal of Special Education,* 31(4), 184–90.

See also: Code of Practice; whole-school policy

EDUCATIONAL PSYCHOLOGIST

Educational psychologists carry out a wide range of tasks in education, although their most frequent involvement is in the area of SEN. They carry out a wide range of tasks aimed at supporting children's learning, and they work with teachers to develop interventions to address learning difficulties. Traditionally, educational psychologists were principally involved in assessing the SEN of individual children and then making recommendations to teachers on how their identified needs might best be met. This role had developed in special education partly as a result of historical factors. In the early part of the twentieth century, psychology was a new and emergent science, which rapidly grew in influence. For example, the old **categories of SEN** largely resulted from the work of medical doctors and psychologists. More recently, and especially following the **Education Act 1981**, which set out statutory requirements for statements and reviews of SEN, educational psychologists continued in a pre-eminent position, often being the key decision makers in the process. A recent government review of their working practices (2005) has meant that the role of educational psychologists has come under scrutiny, with a significant shift to a more consultative approach. The report noted in particular that the professional training and background in psychology, together with their influential position within education, enables educational psychologists to make a substantive and distinctive contribution to the development of **children's services**. This will undoubtedly be influenced by another of the review's recommendations: that educational psychology moves to becoming an all-doctorate profession by 2020.

Most educational psychologists normally work as part of a local authority's educational psychology service, itself part of a children's services provision. As such they provide assessment, consultation, advice and training to early years settings, schools, families and the local authority in general. In particular, they assess the SEN of children and advise teachers and schools on how those needs should be met. In doing this, their activities range from working with an individual pupil to working with groups of teachers or whole schools in a consultative capacity.

Educational psychologists provide support for children and young people who have a wide range of SEN. This can include behavioural difficulties, children having problems with particular aspects of learning (such as reading), children with medical problems that affect their learning, children with hearing or visual impairment, children who may be anxious or withdrawn, and children who are at risk of **exclusion**. They sometimes work directly with an individual pupil or with groups of pupils. At other times they carry out classroom observations to support assessments at **School Action Plus**. The emphasis on this activity is increasingly on **professional collaboration** with teachers and other professionals.

An important function of the educational psychologist, and one which increasingly denotes a more contemporary way of working, is that of facilitation of training activities for teachers in schools, as well as for parents, governors and other professional groups linked to the school. They also provide advice to schools on setting up or reviewing their **whole-school SEN policy**.

Discussion point/question: Are educational psychologists most useful when they work directly with pupils or when they operate as consultants, advising teachers about SEN issues?

Further reading

Atkinson, C., Regan, T. and Williams, C. (2006) 'Working collaboratively with teachers to promote effective learning', *Support for Learning*, 21(1), 33–9.

See also: identification and assessment; statement of SEN

HEALTH VISITOR

A health visitor is a qualified and registered nurse or midwife who is specially trained to assess the health needs of individuals, families and the wider community. They aim to promote good health and prevent illness in the community by offering practical help and advice. Often it is the health wisitor who will signal a particular concern regarding a child, particularly if the child's developmental milestones are not being achieved. Hence, he or she is a major figure in early intervention, which is a crucial requirement in SEN practice.

The role of the health visitor in SEN has been established over many years, and was well illustrated by the Portage approach in early years education. This was a home-based early intervention service for developmentally delayed preschool children, in which the health visitor was centrally involved in helping to train parents to teach their own children.

Health visitors are qualified nurses with further specialised training and are experienced in child health, health promotion and health education. They usually function as part of the National Health Service community health services, working closely with general practitioners, school nurses, midwives, social workers, teachers and other professionals who contribute to **children's services**.

The work of health visitors is varied, and can involve advising new parents about feeding concerns, safety, and the physical and emotional development of the child, as well as about immunisation and general health issues. They also contribute to or help run child-health programmes and parenting groups.

Their role in respect of SEN is quite crucial, inasmuch as they have early contact with families and are thus in a position to identify children who might potentially be at risk. They play a vital role in a range of government initiatives to tackle child poverty and social exclusion, such as Sure Start, and they work in close collaboration with other aspects of children's services including (for example) social services, doctors and probation officers.

Discussion point/question: Is the involvement of a health visitor more crucial in some cases of SEN than in others? Can you give examples?

Further reading

Sturmey, P. and Crisp, A. (1986) 'Portage guide to early education: A review of research', *Educational Psychology*, 6(2), 139–57.

See also: support services

HOME–SCHOOL RELATIONSHIP

The relationship between home and school has long been recognised as vital to the educational progress of all children. The generic literature on education makes consistent reference to it, whilst there is now a substantial body of specialist material solely on this issue. Historically this has not always been the case. Up until about 50 years ago the relationship between schools and the home was very hierarchical and procedural. Contact between home and school tended to be much less frequent than is now current, and the main point of parent–teacher contact was usually at 'parents evenings', when teachers would deliver a summary report on a child's progress. Of course, the means by which parents could communicate with schools was much more limited than now, with fewer domestic telephones, no mobile telephony, email or the internet. In spite of the relatively low level of home–school contact, there was an 'agreed understanding' that parents supported the school and its teachers in the work they undertook.

Significant changes have taken place in the period post 1960. Greater awareness of research showing the benefits of good home–school relations was partly responsible, but there was also a change in the relationship dynamic between the two groups. The latter was, in part, influenced by such initiatives as the community education movement in the 1970s and by a number of influential government reports proclaiming the benefits of good home–school links.

In SEN a trigger for developing more fruitful relationships between parents and teachers arrived with the findings of the **Warnock Report** and their incorporation within the **Education Act 1981**. Warnock, in an influential chapter entitled 'Parents as partners', proposed that parents should become more active participants in making decisions regarding their child's education. Moreover, Warnock suggested that this central role should be enshrined in some form of statutory requirement. As a result of this the Education Act 1981 placed explicit requirements on schools and local authorities regarding how parents should be enabled to participate more fully.

Subsequently it has become apparent that home–school partnerships can often be found in their most developed form in relation to SEN issues. This in many respects is understandable. The parents of a child with complex needs can become very knowledgeable about their child's requirements. Wolfendale (1987), writing of the rationale for involving parents in assessment, refers to their 'equivalent expertise'. There is much to suggest that practitioners stand to be more informed professionals if they form close partnerships with parents. In fact, when children have complex needs, professionals find that they *must* consult with parents in order to understand and make provision for those needs.

The 1990s onwards have marked the culmination of a drive to place schools at the heart of a market-led view of educational provision in England. Crucial to this has been the role of parents, who are now seen as the 'consumers' of a service product. Research relating to aspects of home–school relations in general has been prevalent during the last 15 or so years (Wolfendale, 1999), whilst there is now a body of research that can be drawn on which highlights the growing tension between choice and the marketplace as it relates to pupils with learning difficulties. The current preoccupation with 'inclusive education' in England highlights the importance given to the role of parents, with the Index for Inclusion identifying 15 indicators relating to parental/carer involvement which might be descriptive of a developing 'inclusive culture' (CSIE, 2000).

The marketisation of education following the **Education Act 1988** has led to tension between *choice* (for parents) and *efficiency and effectiveness* (for schools), especially regarding SEN. Halstead (1994) has provided an analysis of likely outcomes of 'freedom of choice' in education, especially as it impacts on parents. He has argued that three dominant perspectives obtain: (i) neo-conservatism: choice as a response to declining standards, resulting in the reintroduction of selection; (ii) neo-liberal: open enrolment results in good schools thriving and others being forced to improve; (iii) pluralism: diversity of provision protects the interests of the child. But individual freedom of choice does not necessarily benefit all individuals in society. These perspectives have been readily recognised within the field of SEN (Lunt and Norwich, 1999). Choices made by some parents (notably the articulate middle class), and by schools themselves, will ensure that some schools attract a greater number of more 'able', socially skilled and motivated pupils at the expense of those who perform less well academically and socially. Concomitant to this is that those schools which attract the former pupils will attract more pupils (thereby becoming increasingly financially viable and increasingly selective – thus maintaining a non-inclusive approach to SEN pupils in particular).

In spite of these tensions and concerns, the relationships between home and school in the field of SEN have become even more vital, as the opportunities for parents to be involved in supporting their child's learning have increased. For example, parents are entitled to be involved in the development of their child's **individual education plan**. In the area of emotional and behavioural difficulties, home–school contracts are sometimes used to enable parents to have direct involvement in the strategies introduced to modify inappropriate behaviour by their child. And **parent partnerships**, throughout England, are evidence of the current level of recognition that SEN are best tackled by dialogue with, and support from, the home.

Discussion point/question: How can a school compensate in cases where the parents of an SEN pupil are unwilling or unable to be involved in home–school links in support of their child?

Further reading

Russell, F. (2003) 'The expectations of parents of disabled children', *British Journal of Special Education*, 30(3), 144–9.

See also: parent partnership

INITIAL TEACHER TRAINING

The development of a set of **professional development national standards** for 'qualified teacher status' (QTS) in 2002 (later to be refined in 2007) represented the culmination of a growth in awareness that all teachers needed to have a basic set of knowledge, understanding and professional skills about SEN, irrespective of where these pupils are taught and at what level. The 'QTS standards' now contain the important requirements that all trainee teachers have to demonstrate that they have the basic skills necessary to recognise when a pupil is failing to achieve, and that they know the procedures for seeking additional classroom help in such cases.

In the early development of special education in England, teachers were trained specifically to work solely with children with SEN. This was most likely to result in a teaching career in a separate **special school** or institution, reflecting the segregated nature of SEN provision in the period prior to the late 1970s. But it was also the case that many adults working with children who had serious SEN did not have a teaching qualification, whilst those that did had no additional specialist skills in SEN.

The **Warnock Report** recommended that all initial teacher training (ITT) courses should contain coverage of SEN. It especially noted the importance of ensuring that new teachers develop the necessary observation skills (crucial in the **assessment** of SEN), and an awareness of the developmental stages of children (important in determining whether a child's development was inconsistent with their chronological age). The report also stressed that trainees should develop skills in modifying and **differentiating** the curriculum for SEN pupils, whilst also becoming aware of the additional support in meeting SEN that was likely to be available to them.

The focus on SEN in ITT has gathered pace over the last 30 or more years, in part because of a growing awareness promoted by the Warnock Report that in most **mainstream schools** as many as 20 per cent of all pupils (and in some schools, far more) will experience learning difficulties at some stage or other during their school career. Moreover, the moves towards integration, then **inclusion**, from the 1980s has increased the likelihood that newly qualified teachers will encounter SEN pupils very early in their teaching career.

As a result of these influences, the 2007 national professional standards for QTS incorporate express requirements to cater for pupils with SEN. Standard 19, for example, requires that all trainees 'know how to make effective personalised provision for those they teach, including those for whom English is an additional language or who have special educational needs or disabilities, and how to take practical account of diversity and promote equality and inclusion in their teaching'. Support for trainees in achieving this standard is provided via dedicated training materials and web-based resources.

ITT provision for SEN is not without its controversies and debates. One of the major issues in ITT relating to SEN has been the demise of specialist ITT courses aimed at those trainees who saw their careers as exclusively being directed towards the most severely disabled pupils in schools – such pupils were often educated exclusively in special schools. In 1984 the Advisory Committee on the Supply and Education of Teachers recommended that all such specialist provision be phased out, and by the end of the 1990s all such provision had ceased. The argument was that all teachers should have a basic qualification in teaching in mainstream settings; those who then wished to embark on further training could do so, using their awareness of teaching and learning in ordinary schools as a baseline. Many commentators argue that such an approach, although consistent with integrated or inclusive education, has led to the loss of professional expertise and skills in very distinct areas of need.

A further dilemma has been that, given the acknowledged complexities of many SEN and the relatively short period of training available to students (most ITT courses now comprise a one-year programme), only a superficial coverage of SEN can be provided. This raises important issues with regard to the level of preparedness of some trainees, and places particular importance on the need for them to undertake additional training in the form of continuing professional development.

On a more positive note, the Training and Development Agency, which has the overall responsibility for the generic training of school teachers in England, has commissioned a set of resources for SEN which are intended to support all training providers. It has also sponsored several innovations in training practice over the last few years, in response to concerns regarding the coverage of SEN in ITT courses.

Discussion point/question: How much time do you think is devoted to the coverage of SEN during initial teacher training? Is this about right, or do you think there ought to be more? Try to find out what the real picture is.

Further reading

Garner, P. (2000) 'Pretzel only policy? Inclusion and the real world of teacher education', *British Journal of Special Education*. 27(3), 111–6.

See also: professional development national standards

LEARNING MENTOR

Learning mentors work mainly in primary and secondary education settings. They provide both academic and pastoral support to SEN pupils. They originated as part of the **Excellence in Cities** initiative (1999–2006), which was a programme designed to help raise the attainment of disadvantaged pupils in the most disadvantaged cities, towns and rural areas in England. They are one of the key groups working with pupils in schools in these locations to address barriers to learning. It follows that many of the pupils they encounter will experience SEN.

Learning mentors are now established as an important occupational group, and they have a set of standards which proscribe the kind and quality of work they undertake. The official government description of their role is to provide 'support and guidance to children, young people and those engaged with them, by removing barriers to learning in order to promote effective participation, enhance individual learning, raise aspirations and achieve full potential'. Their involvement is very much geared to building positive relationships with the pupils they interact with, as well as to liaise with other agencies to ensure that these pupils benefit from an extended support network.

Learning mentors carry out a range of tasks, and work with pupils with wide-ranging ability levels and SEN. Much of their work is directed towards providing one-to-one inputs or small-group work. The focus of these activities may include developing coping strategies, enhancing motivation, raising aspirations and encouraging re-engagement in learning, taking account of a range of complex underlying issues that may impact negatively on learning and achievement (e.g. bereavement, lack of confidence/low self-esteem, low aspirations, mental-health issues, relationship difficulties, bullying, peer pressure, family issues/concerns).

Evaluations of the role by the Office for Standards in Education, Children's Services and Skills (Ofsted) in 2003 has indicated that learning mentors have made a significant impact on the attendance, behaviour, self-esteem and progress of the pupils they support. For example, Ofsted indicate that 95 per cent of schools participating in the Excellence in Cities programme regard their learning mentor activities as making a positive contribution to the school as a whole and to the targeted pupils in particular.

Subsequently learning mentors have now become established as an integral part of the so-called 'children's workforce'.

Discussion point/question: Is the use of mentors and other forms of additional classroom support in SEN simply a means of saving on the cost of employing a fully qualified teacher?

Further reading

Malik, A. (2008) 'A day in the life of a primary mentor', *Extended Schools Update*, February, London: DCSF.

See also: support services; professional support

OCCUPATIONAL THERAPIST

Occupational therapists work with children who have a physical disability, a medical condition, a mental-health problem or a learning disability. Their role is principally to assist them to deal with practical, day-to-day tasks which their disability or SEN prevents them from undertaking. Ultimately the aim of an occupational therapist is to enable children to function as independent learners in school. They work closely with other agencies, including health, social work, housing and educational services.

The role of an occupational therapist is to assist children who have physical, mental health or social difficulties to make adaptations so that they can have more control over their environment. The role is highly 'person centred', and comprises a range of therapeutic interventions for pupils with SEN. These include such things as the development of individual life skills like washing, preparing and eating meals, shopping and transport. Their work can also relate to training in the use of domestic equipment or making adaptations to it in order to enable the pupils to be able to live a fulfilled and inclusive life. Occupational therapists may also assist in developing access opportunities to leisure and social activities for pupils with SEN as well as working at enhancing their skills in interacting with others.

Occupational therapists work with pupils who experience a wide range of SEN. These might include those with physical conditions such as congenital heart disease, children in hospital, a wide variety of physically disabled children (for example, wheelchair users) and pupils with mental-health problems. A further example of the range of work they undertake is their involvement with older pupils with learning difficulties, who may encounter problems in managing money for instance.

In common with other professionals who contribute to children's services, occupational therapists engage in professional collaboration with others, including doctors, social workers, **physiotherapists** and volunteers, as well as parents.

Discussion point/question: Try to find out more about the range of services provided by an occupational therapist. Which SEN are they most likely to be involved with?

Further reading

Rodger, S. and Ziviani, J. (1999) 'Play-based occupational therapy', *Disability, Development and Education*, 46(3), 337–65.

See also: health visitor; Every Child Matters

PARENT PARTNERSHIP

Closely linked to the concept of **home–school relationships** is another form of parent–education interface: the 'parent partnership'. Whilst the idea of a partnership between parents and educational professionals is well established, having been around for many years, the notion of a formal national arrangement for all parents is a relatively recent concept. In the late 1970s the **Warnock Report** reviewed provision for children with SEN in England and Wales. The report contained an influential chapter entitled 'Parents as partners', and this was one of the influences in setting in motion a more consistent and structured approach to relationships with parents.

Parent partnerships themselves were first introduced by the New Labour government in the late 1990s, and are located in every local authority (LA) area in England. Similar arrangements are in place in the rest of the UK. Their importance is especially to provide support to parents of children with SEN. The former can sometimes be socially isolated, especially in cases where the SEN is a very uncommon, or 'low-incidence' need.

Parent partnerships are statutory services that offer information, advice and support for parents (the term is taken also to include principal carers) of children and young people with SEN. They also act as a pivotal point for collating local and national contact points for parents, and, as such, are able to put them in touch with other local organisations and groups which can provide support on SEN issues. Parent partnerships also have a role in making sure that parent's views are heard and understood and that these views inform local policy and practice. This is particularly important given the social marginalisation of some communities and minority groups with an over-representation of SEN.

Some parent partnerships are based in the voluntary sector although the majority are located in LA or children's trusts. Importantly, all parent partnerships, wherever they are based, are independent of the LA and are thus able to provide impartial advice and support to parents.

In total there are 147 parent partnerships in England at the present time (November 2008).

Discussion point/question: Can official mechanisms such as parent partnerships realistically do anything to support those parents who are under extreme stress as a result of psychological, emotional, social or economic difficulties? Are such parents the least able to make use of statutory, government-supported resources like parent partnerships?

Further reading

Rogers, R., Tod, J., Powell, S., Parsons, C., Godfrey, R., Graham-Matheson, L., Carlson, A. and Cornwall, J. (2006) *Evaluation of the Special Educational Needs Parent Partnership Service in England*. London: DCSF.

See also: home–school relationship

PHYSIOTHERAPIST

The role of physiotherapists is to assist children's mobility, posture and physical condition by carrying out physical treatments. They are employed by the National Health Service and are based either in hospitals or in community health centres. They also visit schools and other educational settings. Physiotherapy is a branch of health care which regards human movement as central to the health and well-being of children. Physiotherapists work with a range of pupils who have SEN or disabilities. As with other professional roles, theirs has been subject to operational changes: physiotherapists increasingly work in a consultative capacity, providing both ongoing assessment of pupils as well as advice and training to teachers and **teaching assistants**. To qualify as a physiotherapist requires completion of an honours degree (BSc in physiotherapy) which covers areas such as anatomy, physiology, physics and pathology, as well as ethical and child-protection issues relating to physically handling children.

Working with other professionals is an essential feature of the role of physiotherapists; it is seen as essential that physiotherapists have good communication skills, as this work brings them into close physical contact with pupils, as well as other key professionals.

Discussion point/question: Where can a teacher or teaching assistant obtain more information about the inter-professional role of a physiotherapist?

Further reading

Parkes, J., Hill, N., Dolk, H. and Donelly, M. (2004) 'What influences physiotherapy use by children with cerebral palsy?', *Child: Care, Health and Development*, 30(2), 151–60.

See also: support services

PROFESSIONAL COLLABORATION

The complex nature of many SEN has resulted in the development of inter-agency working between representatives from a wide range of professions – particularly from education, health, social services, police and youth justice. This approach has long been advocated as representing 'good practice' in meeting the needs of pupils and has reached a point of considerable refinement in the reorganisation of local authority (LA) arrangements for education within an overarching children's-services provision. This reflects the policy requirements of both the **Every Child Matters** guidance as well as that of the Children's Agenda, exemplified by such initiatives as the '**team around the child**'. Professional collaboration is also sometimes referred to as multidisciplinary or multi-agency working.

The **Warnock Report** advocated the importance of professional collaboration, and this way of working is a salient feature of a school's response to SEN, especially where the level of seriousness of the learning difficulty is confirmed. The last 30 years has seen both a confirmation of the importance of existing professional teamwork (good examples of this are the Schools Psychology Service and the speech and language service within LAs) and the development of new professional groupings (for instance, the child and adolescent mental-health services).

The most obvious example of professional collaboration is in SEN provision at **School Action Plus**, and that part of the provision which leads to a **statement** of SEN being made for a child. In cases like these a **class teacher, special educational needs coordinator** (SENCO), parent or **educational psychologist**, together with (dependent on the nature of the SEN) a paediatrician, **speech therapist** and so on, would be involved in determining an educa- tional plan for the child. 'Multi-professional **assessment**' is an integral component of SEN provision in cases where the level of seriousness of the learning difficulty is such that special arrangements need to be made to meet these needs. The advantage of this process is that each member of the group clearly brings distinct skills and sets of professional knowledge.

There has been considerable raising of awareness of professional teamwork in schools. Most teachers now recognise that pupils with SEN may need additional support, and are accustomed to working alongside other professionals in their classrooms. Moreover, the range of professions involved in providing services for SEN has dramatically increased. One recent survey of behaviour support for pupils with **emotional and behavioural difficulties** has indicated over 40 separate professional groups who may, at one point or another, come in contact with a pupil who presents serious challenging behaviour.

Of course, such inter-professional collaboration brings with it a range of potential pitfalls, along with its advantages. One of these is the high costs involved in bring together groups of highly paid professionals. Another drawback is that there might well be professional tensions regarding such matters as confidentiality, interpretation of assessment data and even the existence of either overt or tacit professional hierarchies.

In spite of these issues the benefits of professional collaboration in SEN are immense. Recognition of the positive impact of this way of working on the child is highly apparent when one considers recent policy developments in SEN. The Children's Agenda is most definitely underpinned by close professional collaboration to provide support and resources for all children in schools. Those with SEN are particular beneficiaries.

Discussion point/question: Consider just one SEN from the illustrative list contained in this book. Besides a teacher and SENCO, what other professionals are likely to be involved with the pupil?

Further reading

Todd, L. (2006) *Partnerships for Inclusive Education: A Critical Approach to Collaborative Working*. London: Routledge.

See also: Every Child Matters; professional collaboration

PROFESSIONAL DEVELOPMENT NATIONAL STANDARDS

One of the most important developments in training and professional awareness relating to SEN during the last ten years has been the establishment of sets of national professional standards for teachers in **mainstream** and **special schools**. The standards comprise SEN-specific requirements for teachers which refer to: (a) the role of the **special educational needs coordinator** (SENCO); (b) the work of teachers working with pupils who have profound, severe and complex SEN; and (c) those teachers who work in the area of hearing impairment, visual impairment or multi-sensory impairment. The latter group of standards are mandatory.

The national standards have been developed by the Training and Development Agency. The purpose of the standards is to ensure that as teachers in mainstream schools encounter an increasingly diverse range of SEN pupils because of the impact of **inclusion** policies, they are better equipped to teach them so that they have maximum access to the curriculum and are fully included in the life of the school. The national standards (apart from those which are mandatory – see below) can be achieved by teachers following a recognised programme of study, usually provided by an institution of higher education, local authority or designated independent provider.

The national standards for SENCOs set out the professional knowledge, skills and attributes needed to carry out the role effectively. The standards assume that the teacher appointed as a SENCO will have a substantial background in and knowledge of SEN. The SENCO standards focus specifically on recognising and further developing the teacher's expertise in leadership and management and comprise five sections:

1. The core purpose of the SENCO
2. Key outcomes of SEN coordination
3. Professional knowledge and understanding

4. Skills and attributes
5. Key areas of SEN coordination

The specialist standards are divided into four parts. The first covers more generic aspects of working with pupils who have SEN, and involves such things as identification, **assessment** and planning, effective teaching, the development of communication, literacy and numeracy skills, and the promotion of social and emotional development. These are known as the 'core standards'.

The second part, referred to as the 'extension standards', relates to the knowledge, skills and professional attributes necessary for effective working with pupils who have SEN in the four groupings of learning difficulty identified in the SEN **Code of Practice**, namely:

- communication and interaction;
- cognition and learning;
- behaviour, emotional and social development;
- sensory and/or physical needs.

Third, the specialist standards provide details of the role of specialist advisory personnel and those functioning in a managerial capacity.

In relation to the national standards for teachers working with children who have hearing, visual or multi-sensory impairments, the Education (School Teachers' Qualifications) (England) Regulations (2003) stipulate that a specialist qualification is necessary. In addition to holding qualified teacher status, a teacher working with such pupils must possess a qualification approved by the Secretary of State. A number of higher education institutions – known as mandatory providers – are approved to award this specialist qualification.

Discussion point/question: Should any set of national standards which help demonstrate a teacher's skills and aptitudes in the field of SEN be linked to career progression and pay?

Further reading

Garner, P. and Lewis, G. (1999) 'Standardising teachers: Attitudes towards national standards for those working with children with learning difficulties', *Early Child Development and Care*, 157, 97–107.

See also: initial teacher training

PROFESSIONAL SUPPORT

Because there are many underlying causes of SEN, covering a wide range of disciplines (including, for example, medicine, psychology and social interaction), it follows that professional support is not provided just by one individual or professional grouping. Professional support for pupils with SEN has long been recognised as an essential part of provision. Government reports dating back over 50 years have advocated greater involvement of a wide range of professionals. The reliance on a range of professions to address SEN, rather than solely educationists in schools, has been illustrated in the most recent SEN-related legislation. The **Children's Plan** highlights the need for a variety of professionals, each with their own background, expertise and skills, to make inputs to the educational experience of pupils who encounter learning difficulties.

A clue to the extent that schools now rely on other professional groups to enhance their work with SEN pupils is to be found in the statutory and non-statutory documentation currently in use in delivering education to SEN pupils. The **individual education plan**, for example, requires that, where appropriate, observations and inputs can be made by a range of professionals – **educational psychologists**, social workers, therapists, medical doctors, psychiatrists and so on. One recent example of the number of professional groups involved in attending to a given SEN is the case of pupils with **emotional and behavioural difficulties** (EBDs). In a commissioned survey of the EBD workforce, over 40 separate groups were identified as potential professional stakeholders. This included teachers, learning mentors, psychiatrists, social workers, education welfare workers, educational psychologists, police officers, probation officers, **family therapists** and so on.

Each professional group brings particular knowledge and skills to play in addressing the learning needs of pupils – a further indication of the complexity of many SEN in terms of their aetiology. No single professional can be adequately skilled or prepared to cater for the multidimensional nature of many SEN. So it is vital that the expertise of the whole professional community is sought. Current evidence is widespread that such multi-**professional collaboration** is crucial to effectively meeting the needs of children with SEN.

Discussion point/question: Do you think that there are possible difficulties in defining specific professional roles in inter-agency work? What possible tensions might this give rise to?

Further reading

Glenny, G. (2005) 'Riding the dragon: Developing inter-agency systems for supporting inclusion', *Support for Learning*, 20(4), 167–75.

See also: support services

SCHOOL GOVERNOR (SEN)

Every school in England has a governing body, whose principal duty is the effective delivery of high-quality education for all pupils, irrespective of their level of educational attainment. The governing body is required to nominate one of its members to act in the role of the governor responsible for SEN. The role of this governor is to maintain an overview of the types of SEN within the school, noting the balance between the numbers of pupils with specific types of SEN in order to provide a summary of this situation to the school's governing body and advise on any likely resource implications. The SEN governor, liaising with the **special educational needs coordinator**, will monitor the financial implications for the school's budget, and offer guidance on the school's use of any SEN-specific monies delegated from the local authority (LA).

The role of a school's governing body, including its nominated SEN governor, is set out in the 2001 **Code of Practice**. This states that the governing body has certain responsibilities, including the following duties:

- Do its best to ensure that the necessary provision is made for any pupil who has SEN.
- Ensure that, where the 'responsible person' – the head teacher or the appropriate governor – has been informed by the LA that a pupil has SEN, those needs are made known to all who are likely to teach him or her.
- Ensure that teachers in the school are aware of the importance of identifying and providing for those pupils who have SEN.
- Ensure that a pupil with SEN joins in the activities of the school together with pupils who do not have SEN, so far as is reasonably practical and compatible with the child receiving the special educational provision their learning needs call for and the efficient education of the pupils with whom they are educated, as well as the efficient use of resources.

Discussion point/question: Does a school's SEN governor need to be a person who has 'insider knowledge' of the topic, or simply somebody with a significant commitment to SEN?

Further reading

Adams, J. (2004) *Governing not Managing: Governing Body Annual Responsibility Survey*, NAGM Research Report No.18. Birmingham: NAGM. Also at www.nagm.org.uk/research.html (accessed 10 July 2008).

See also: Code of Practice

SEN TRIBUNAL

The Education Act 1993 established the Special Educational Needs and Disability Tribunal. Its role is to consider those cases when parents appeal against the decisions of a local authority (LA) regarding the SEN provision that it will make for a child with learning difficulties and where the parents are unable to resolve matters with the LA. The Tribunal is independent and its decisions cannot be influenced by central government or by any LA.

Official statistics show that appeals to the Tribunal have increased from just over 1000 in 1995 to just over 3000 ten years later. The most recent figures available show that in February 2008 the Tribunal considered 271 individual cases, and of these 123 were 'conceded by the local authority'. These statistics also show that in 84 cases the parents actually withdrew the appeal prior to it being fully considered by the Tribunal.

The SEN Tribunal has very particular powers and can require LAs to make significant changes to their previous decisions regarding provision for a child with a learning difficulty or disability. Some examples of these show the extent of the importance of this role. In cases where the LA has refused to make a **statement**, the Tribunal can order it to do so if it is viewed by it as being necessary for the effective education of the child. But the Tribunal cannot influence the actual wording of a new statement, although it can require changes to be made when parents appeal about the provision described in an existing statement.

Discussion point/question: Why do you think that parents might withdraw an appeal to an SEN Tribunal?

Further reading

Soar, K., Gersch, I. and Lawrence, A. (2006) 'Pupil involvement in special educational needs disagreement resolution: A parental perspective', *Support for Learning,* 21(3), 149–55.

See also: home–school relationship; parent partnership

SPECIAL EDUCATIONAL NEEDS COORDINATOR

The special educational needs coordinator (SENCO) was identified in the 1994 SEN **Code of Practice** as the key person in a school responsible for the organisation, management and coordination of SEN provision. Since that time the SENCO role has become established as the point of reference for all matters relating to the day-to-day operation of the requirements set out in the revised Code of Practice (2001).

In many schools the SENCO is a member of the 'school leadership team' and as such is in a position to influence strategic planning and policy decisions regarding SEN. As such the SENCO role has developed from a utilitarian one of 'coordination' to a more leadership-orientated function. This change is a hallmark of the increasing level of sophistication in the way that SENCOs now operate. What is worth noting is that it is not necessarily the case that the SENCO is a qualified teacher, although more usually this is the situation. An experienced **teaching assistant** can have the appropriate range of skills to be able to fill the role, although this is more inclined to be the case in some small primary schools. It is also worth recognising that some schools prefer to use alternative titles for the role covered by the SENCO. Some settings, for example, use the term 'inclusion coordinator' or 'INCO', a decision based on the belief that the focus on provision should not be placed on a separate set of procedures which seem to reinforce difference, but should be placed on promoting inclusive practices which apply to all irrespective of their needs.

The responsibilities of the SENCO are widespread and important. In some larger schools an assistant SENCO is identified to share these duties. Moreover, the role involves as much interaction between the SENCO and other adults (teachers, teaching assistants, **educational psychologists**, **speech therapists**, parents and so on) as it does with children and young people. In many large schools, especially secondary schools, some SENCOs have no direct teaching responsibility, an issue which brings with it a number of dilemmas – most notably the fact that they are often the most experienced teachers in respect of SEN children in the school and yet their skills are not being used directly in working with the pupils.

Typically the job description of a SENCO covers four aspects of work, each of considerable importance in supporting the educational progress of children with SEN. First, they have responsibility for managing all matters relating to teaching and learning. They take the lead in identifying the most effective teaching approaches for pupils with SEN and promoting their adoption by all other staff in the school. They also have a monitoring and evaluation function, helping to ensure that teaching and learning activities are appropriate to meet the needs of pupils with SEN. They also promote the acquisition of appropriate study skills so that SEN pupils can develop the ability to work independently. The SENCO's role is in coordination and leadership, with less direct intervention with children than was previously the case.

Second, the SENCO role has a major focus on recording and **assessment**. As such, the SENCO is involved in ensuring that learning targets are established for all pupils with SEN, and that systems are in place to gather data and evidence which will enable the school to measure the progress that is being made. Gathering data is a vital part of the initial identification and assessment of SEN, as well as being essential for evaluation and the legally binding annual review for all children who hold a **statement** of SEN. As with learning and teaching, the SENCO holds significant responsibility for liaising with other teachers or supporting professionals, as well as with parents.

The leadership function of the SENCO comprises a third major area of responsibility. The role requires that the SENCO encourages all members of the school's teaching and support staff to recognise and fulfil their statutory requirements towards children with SEN. They must also ensure that new statutory guidance and advice from government is made accessible, whilst providing opportunities for staff training and development in the area of SEN and **inclusion**.

Finally, the SENCO has a responsibility for quality assurance and the overall standard of SEN provision. Although the ultimate responsibility rests with the school governors and head teacher, the SENCO has to make sure that what the school does to support all children with SEN is consistent with what is recognised as 'good practice'.

A national set of 'SENCO standards' has been developed to assist the process of ensuring that uniformity is achieved in coordinating the various functions of the SENCO (TTA, 1999). Whilst these national professional standards are not statutory, many SENCOs use them as guidelines to evaluate their work.

Discussion point/question: In most schools is the role of the SENCO too broad and complex to be in the hands of just one person?

Further reading

Layton, L. (2005) 'Special educational needs coordinators and leadership: A role too far?', *Support for Learning*, 20(2), 53–60.

See also: Code of Practice

SPEECH AND LANGUAGE THERAPIST

Many children experience SEN related to speech, language and communication problems. These can range from a difficulty producing and using speech or a difficulty understanding language to a difficulty in actually using language. The source of the communication problem might be linked to a physiological (for example, cleft palate) or psychological/physiological issue (as, for example, in the case of stammering). Speech therapists also work closely with children who have hearing impairments and with some who have neurological or psychological problems.

The role of a speech and language therapist is to assess the seriousness of these conditions, and to advise teachers, parents and other professionals (including **educational psychologists** and doctors) on how best to enable these children to communicate more effectively with others.

As well as working in schools (both **mainstream** and **special settings**), speech therapists are also located in hospitals, health centres and day centres run by social services departments.

Training to be a speech and language therapist involves completion of an honours degree in speech and language therapy. The course covers a range of theory and practice in a range of areas, including language pathology and therapeutics, speech and language sciences, behavioural sciences, biomedical sciences, education, acoustics, psychology, sociology and professional issues. The practical component of the degree programme ensures that, once trained, the speech therapist is able to utilise a set of clinical skills in a variety of settings and levels of pupil need.

The publishing of the **Bercow Report** in mid-2008 has acted as a stimulus to the discussion regarding the importance of the role of the speech and language therapist.

Discussion point/question: Why do schools sometimes find it difficult to access the services of a speech and language therapist in working with an SEN child?

Further reading

Lindsay, G. and Dockrell, J. (2002) 'Meeting the needs of children with speech, language and communication needs: A critical perspective on inclusion and collaboration', *Child Language Teaching and Therapy*, 18, 91–101.

See also: categories of SEN

TEACHING ASSISTANT

Only a very short time ago (maybe 15 or so years) the concept of a 'teaching assistant' was a relatively new one in many schools. Classroom assistants were frequently used up until around 1999–2000, but they had little official status in schools, even though the work they undertook was immensely valuable. Moreover, they were traditionally very lowly paid and worked on term-time only contracts, often without full employee benefits. The arrival of the 'remodelling agenda', which meant that schools had to examine the ways in which staff were utilised, resulted in wholesale changes and the gradual 'professionalisation' of 'classroom assistants' into teaching assistants – now widely referred to as TAs – and, later on, 'higher-level teaching assistants', or HLTAs.

Whilst TAs do not necessarily work exclusively with pupils who have SEN, they nevertheless do need an awareness regarding learning difficulties. Moreover, it is the case that many TAs are allocated to support pupils with SEN, often as a statutory element of the child's **statement**. In all cases there are important issues relating to levels of training and of the need to ensure effective collaborative working between the TA and the **class teacher**.

One of the most significant developments in recent years, associated directly with the professionalisation of this part of the school's workforce, has been the establishment of sets of national standards for TAs and HLTAs. The widespread application of these has led to a significant rise in the perceived status of this group of workers.

One development which has contributed to this increase in standing within education has been the central position that TAs have secured in the government's workforce remodelling agenda. One of the driving principles behind this has been an acceptance that the role of the teacher in schools has changed in the twenty-first century. Teachers in contemporary England have become facilitators of learning, enabling their pupils to access knowledge in a variety of ways. The traditional version of the 'teacher', who holds a corpus of knowledge and distributes this to pupils according to an agreed protocol and timetable, is no longer applicable in the 'knowledge society'. Teachers have become classroom 'leaders', directing the way pupils learn rather than necessarily determining what they learn. TAs now provide an essential role in providing support to teachers by providing services and resources which free them (the teachers) to direct the learning of pupils with SEN.

Discussion point/question: What kinds of issue would the teacher and TA need to discuss prior to a lesson if the latter was to be able to offer effective support to a pupil with SEN?

Further reading

Watkinson, A. (2008) *The Essential Guide for Competent Teaching Assistants.* London: David Fulton.

See also: professional collaboration; classroom teacher

BIBLIOGRAPHY

The literature on SEN is vast and is growing virtually by the day. The following books, journal articles and pamphlets have been used by practitioners and researchers alike over the last 10–15 years. I have selected them both to illustrate further the concepts included in this volume and also to provide readers with a glimpse of the sheer variety of resources that now exist for those wishing to explore the generic topic of SEN in greater detail.

For the purposes of this bibliography, I have divided the references into two sections. The first comprises generic books on SEN: these books cover such issues as philosophies, policies, school organisation, curriculum and teaching in varying levels of detail. The second section provides a set of materials which are topic specific: these deal in greater detail with focus on a specific aspect of SEN.

(i) Bibliography: Generic SEN issues

Ainscow, M. (1997) 'Towards inclusive schooling', *British Journal of Special Education,* 24(1), 3–6.

Armstrong, F., Armstrong, D., and Barton, L. (2002) (eds) *Inclusive Education – Policy, Contexts and Comparative Perspectives.* London: David Fulton.

Babbage, R., Byers, R. and Redding, H. (1999) *Approaches to Teaching and Learning: Including Pupils with Learning Difficulties.* London: David Fulton.

Blamires, M. (1999) *Enabling Technology for Inclusion.* London: Paul Chapman.

Blamires, M. and Moore, J. (2006) *Supporting Services and Mainstream Schools – A Guide for Working Together.* London: David Fulton.

Booth, T. and Ainscow, M. (2002) *The Index of Inclusion.* Bristol: CSIE.

Clough, P. and Barton, L. (1998) (eds) *Articulating with Difficulty – Research Voices in Inclusive Education.* London: Paul Chapman.

Colwill, I. and Peacey, N. (2001) 'Planning, teaching and assessing the curriculum for pupils with learning difficulties: Curriculum guidelines to support the revised National Curriculum', *British Journal of Special Education,* 28(3), 120–2.

Cowie, H. and Wallace, P. (2000) *Peer Support in Action.* London: Sage.

Croll, P. and Moses, D. (2003) 'Special educational needs across two decades: Survey evidence form two primary schools', *British Educational Research Journal*, 29(5), 731–47.

Daniels, H. (ed.) (2000) *Special Education Re-Formed. Beyond Rhetoric?* London: Falmer Press.

Daniels, H. and Garner, P. (eds) 1999) *World Yearbook of Education: Inclusive Education*. London Kogan Page.

Daniels, H. and Ware, J. (1990) *Special Educational Needs and the National Curriculum: The Impact of the Education Reform Act*. The Bedford Way Series. London: Kogan Page.

Dee, L. and Alexander, E. (2002) *Supporting Self-Esteem and Emotional Well-Being among Young People with Learning Disabilities: A Discussion Paper*. London: Mental Health Foundation.

Evans, J. and Lunt, I. (2002) 'Inclusive education: are there limits?', *European Journal of Special Needs Education*, 17(1), 1–14.

Farrell, P. (1997) *Teaching Pupils with Learning Difficulties: Strategies and Solutions*. London: Cassell.

Farrell, P. (2000) 'The impact of research on developments in inclusive education', *International Journal of Inclusive Education*, 4(2), 153–62.

Farrell, P. and Ainscow, M. (2002) (eds) *Making Special Education Inclusive*. London: David Fulton.

Fletcher-Campbell, F. (2001) 'Issues of inclusion: Evidence from three recent research studies', *Emotional and Behavioural Difficulties*, 6(2), 69–89.

Frederickson, N. and Cline, T. (2002) *Special Educational Needs, Inclusion and Diversity: A Textbook*. Buckingham: Open University Press.

Gross, J. and White, A. (2003) *Special Educational Needs and School Improvement*. London: David Fulton.

Hegarty, S. (1993) 'Reviewing the literature on integration', *European Journal of Special Needs Education*, 8(3), 194–200.

Heward, W.L. (2003) 'Ten faulty notions about teaching and learning that hinder the effectiveness of special education', *Journal of Special Education*, 36 (4), 186–205.

Hornby, G., Atkinson, M. and Howard, J. (1997) *Controversial Issues in Special Education*. London: David Fulton.

Jenkinson, J.C. (1997) *Mainstream or Special? Educating Students with Disabilities*. London: Routledge.

Knowles, G. (ed.) (2006) *Supporting Inclusive Practice*. London: David Fulton.

Lewis, A. and Norwich B. (2001) 'Mapping a pedagogy for special educational needs', *British Education Research Journal*, 27(3), 313–29.

Lewis, A. and Norwich B. (2005) *Special Teaching for Special Children?*. Buckingham: Open University Press.

Lunt, I. and Norwich, B. (1999) *Can Effective Schools be Inclusive Schools? Perspectives on Education Policy*. London: Institute of Education, University of London.

McGregor, G. and Vogelsburg, R. (1998) *Inclusive Schooling Practices: Pedagogical and Research Foundations: A Synthesis of the Literature that Informs Best Practices about Inclusive Schooling*. Baltimore: Paul H. Brooks.

Mitchell, D. (ed.) (2004) *Special Educational Needs and Inclusive Education: Major Themes in Education*. London: Routledge Falmer.

Mittler, P. (2000) *Working towards Inclusive Education: Social Contexts*. London: David Fulton.

Mittler, P. (2002) 'Educating pupils with intellectual disabilities in England: Thirty years on', *International Journal of Disability, Development and Education*, 49(2), 145–60.

Munn, P., Lloyd, G. and Cullen, M.A. (2000) *Alternatives to Exclusion from School*. London: Paul Chapman

Nind, M., Rix, J., Sheehy, K. and Simmons, K. (2003) (eds) *Inclusive Education: Diverse Perspectives*. London: David Fulton.

Norwich, B. (2008) *Dilemmas of Difference, Inclusion and Disability: International Perspectives and Future Directions*. London: Routledge.

Papps, I. and Dyson, A. (2004) *The Costs and Benefits of Earlier Identification and Effective Intervention*. London: DfES.

Qualifications and Curriculum Authority (2001) *Planning, Teaching and Assessing the Curriculum for Pupils with Learning Difficulties: Developing Skills*. London: QCA.

Rayner, S. (2007) *Managing Special and Inclusive Education*. London: Sage Publications.

Sebba, J. and Sachdev, D. (1997) *What Works in Inclusive Education?*. Ilford: Bernardos.

Sebba, J., Byers, R. and Rose, R. (1995) *Redefining the Whole Curriculum for Pupils with Learning Difficulties*. London: David Fulton.

Skidmore, D. (1999) 'Continuities and developments in research into the education of pupils with learning difficulties', *British Journal of Educational Studies*, 47(1), 3–16.

Slavin, R. (December 1989/January 1990) 'Research on co-operative learning: consensus and controversy', *Educational Leadership*, 47(4), 52–4.

Slee, R. (2006) 'Critical analyses of inclusive education policy: an international survey', *International Journal of Inclusive Education*, 10(2, 3), 105–7.

Thomas, G. and Loxley, A. (2007) *Deconstructing Special Education and Constructing Inclusion*. 2nd edn. Buckingham: Open University Press.

Tilstone, C., Florian, L. and Rose, R. (1998) *Promoting Inclusive Practice*. London: Routledge.

Vaughan, M. and Thomas, G. (2004) *Inclusive Education – Readings and Reflections*. Buckingham: Open University Press.

Vlachou, A. (1997) *Struggles for Inclusive Education*. Buckingham: Open University Press.

(ii) Bibliography: References used in the text

Adams, J. (2004) *Governing not Managing: Governing Body Annual Responsibility Survey*, NAGM Research Report No.18. Birmingham: NAGM. Also at www.nagm.org.uk/research.html (accessed 10 July 2008).

Alderson, P. and Goodey, C. (1999) 'Autism in special and inclusive schools: There has to be a point to their being there', *Disability & Society*, 14(2), 249–61.

Armstrong, D. (2003) *Experiences of Special Education: Re-Evaluating Policy and Practice through Life Stories*. London: Routledge.

Arroyos-Jurado E., Paulsen J., Merrell K., Lindgren S. and Max J. (2000) 'Traumatic brain injury in school-age children: Academic and social outcome', *Journal of School Psychology*, 38(6), 571–87.

Asprey, A. and Nash, T. (2006) 'The importance of awareness and communication for the inclusion of young people with life-limiting and life-threatening conditions in mainstream schools and colleges', *British Journal of Special Education*, 33(1), 10–18.

Atkinson, C., Regan, T. and Williams, C. (2006) 'Working collaboratively with teachers to promote effective learning', *Support for Learning*, 21(1), 33–9.

Baginsky, M. (2002) *Child Protection and Education*, NSPCC Research Briefing. London: NSPCC.

Banks, P., Cogan, N., Deeley, S., Hill, M., Riddell, S. and Tisdall, K. (2001) 'Seeing the invisible: Children and young people affected by disability', *Disability & Society*, 16(6), 797–814.

Barkley, R., Guevremont, D., Anastopoulos, A. and Fletcher, K. (1992) 'A comparison of three family therapy programs for treating family conflicts in adolescents with attention deficit hyperactivity disorder', *Journal of Consulting and Clinical Psychology*, 60(3) 450–62.

Barton, L. and Tomlinson, S. (1984) *Special Education and Social Interests*. London: Croom Helm.

Bennathan, M. (1997) 'Effective intervention in primary schools: What nurture groups achieve?', *Emotional and Behavioural Difficulties*, 2(3), 23–9.

Berger, A., Henderson, J. and Morris, D. (1999) *Implementing the Literacy Hour for Children with Learning Difficulties*. London: David Fulton.

Beveridge, S. (1999) *Special Educational Needs in Schools*. London: Routledge.

Bird, R. (2007) *The Dyscalculia Toolkit – Supporting Learning Difficulties in Maths*. London: Sage.

Booth T. (1988) 'Challenging conceptions of integration', in Barton L (ed.) *The Politics of Special Educational Needs*. London: Falmer Press, 97–122.

Brodin, J. (2005) 'Diversity of aspects on play in children with profound multiple disabilities', *Early Child Development and Care*, 175, 635–46.

Brooks, G., Flanagan, N., Henkhuzens, Z. and Hutchison, D. (1998) *What Works for Slow Readers? The Effectiveness of Early Intervention Schemes*. Slough, UK: National Foundation for Educational Research.

Carpenter, B. and Morgan, H. (2003) 'Count us in: The role of schools and colleges in meeting the mental-health needs of young people with learning disabilities', *British Journal of Special Education*, 30(4), 202–5.

Chadwick, O., Beecham, J., Piroth, N., Bernard, S. and Taylor, E. (2002) 'Respite care for children with severe intellectual disability and their families: Who needs it? Who receives it?', *Child and Adolescent Mental Health*, 7(2), 66–72.

Cheminais, R. (2006) *Every Child Matters. A Practical Guide for Teachers*. London: David Fulton.

Child, D. (2005) 'Concept formation and cognitive development', in S. Child *Psychology and the Teacher*. London: Continuum, 61–88.

Cline, T. (ed.) (1994) *The Assessment of Special Educational Needs – International Perspectives*. London: Routledge.

Clough, P., Garner, P., Pardeck, T. and Yuen, F. (2005) *The Handbook of Emotional and Behavioural Difficulties*. London: Sage.

Connor, M. (1998) 'A review of behavioural early intervention programmes for children with autism', *Educational Psychology in Practice*, 14, 109–117.

Conti-Ramsden, G. and Botting, N. (2004) 'Social difficulties and victimisation in children with SLI at 11 years of age', *Journal of Speech, Language and Hearing Research*, 47(1), 145–72.

Cooper, C. (2004) '"A struggle well worth having": The uses of theatre-in-education (TIE) for learning', *Support for Learning*, 19(2), 81–7.

Cooper, P. (1993) 'Learning from pupils' perspectives', *British Journal of Special Education*, 20(4), 129–33.

Cooper, P. and O'Regan, F. (2001) *Educating Children with ADHD*. London: Routledge.

Cooper, P., Smith, C. and Upton, G. (1994) *Emotional Behavioural Difficulties: Theory to Practice*. London: Routledge.

Corbett, J. (1996) *Bad Mouthing: The Language of Special Needs*. London: Falmer Press.

Cowne, E. (2005) 'What do special educational needs coordinators think they do?', *Support for Learning*, 20(2), 61–8.

Cowne, E. (2008) *The SENCO Handbook. Working within a Whole-School Approach*. London: Routledge.

Cummings, C., Dyson, A. and Todd, L. (2004) *Evaluation of the Extended Schools Pathfinder Projects*. London: DES.

Daniels, H. and Garner, P. (1999) *The World Yearbook of Education. Inclusive Education*. London: Kogan Page.

Daniels, H., Hey, V., Leonard, D. and Smith, M. (2000) 'Issues of equity in special needs education as seen from the perspective of gender', in H. Daniels (ed.) *Special Education Re-Formed: Beyond Rhetoric?* London: Falmer Press, 47–66.

Davis, P. (2003) *Including Children with Visual Impairment in Mainstream Schools: A Practical Guide*. London: David Fulton.

Deci, E., Vallerand, R., Pelletier, L. and Ryan, R. (1991) 'Motivation and education: The self-determination perspective', *Educational Psychologist*, 26 (3/4), 325–46.

Department for Education and Skills (2005) *Extended Schools: Access to Opportunities and Services for All. A Prospectus*. London: DfES.

Department of Education and Science (1975) *Language for Life*. (The Bullock Report). London: DES.

Department for Children, Schools and Families (2005) *Learning Behaviour* (Steer Report). London: DCSF.

Dos Santos, M. (2001) 'Special education, inclusion and globalisation: A few considerations inspired in the Brazilian case', *Disability and Society*, 16(2), 311–25.

Dyson, A. (1997) 'Social and educational disadvantage: Reconnecting special needs education', *British Journal of Special Education*, 24(4), 152–7.

East Riding Council (2008) 'Provision mapping – An "at a glance" way of showing the range of provision', www.eriding.net/inclusion/provmap_res.shtml (accessed 16 July 2008).

Elliott, J. (1999) 'Practitioner review: School refusal: Issues of conceptualisation, assessment, and treatment', *The Journal of Child Psychology and Psychiatry and Allied Disciplines*, 40, 1001–12.

Essen, J. and Wedge, P. (1982) *Continuities in Childhood Disadvantage*. London: Heinemann.

Farrell, P., Dyson, A., Polat, F., Hutcheson, G. and Gallannaugh, F. (2007) 'The relationship between inclusion and academic achievement in English mainstream schools', *School Effectiveness and School Improvement*, 18(3), 335–52.

Florian, L. (2002) 'The more things change the more they stay the same? A response to the Audit Commission's report on statutory assessment and statements of SEN', *British Journal of Special Education*, 29(4), 164–9.

Florian, L. and Hegarty, S. (2004) *ICT and Special Educational Needs: A Tool for Inclusion*. Buckingham: Open University Press.

Florian, L., Rouse, M. and Black Hawkins, K. (2007) *Achievement and Inclusion in Schools*. London: Routledge.

Fox, S., Farrell, P. and Davis, P. (2004) 'Factors associated with the effective inclusion of primary-aged pupils with Down's syndrome', *British Journal of Special Education,* 31(4), 184–90.

Freeman, L. and Miller, A. (2001) 'Norm-referenced, criterion-referenced, and dynamic assessment: What exactly is the point?', *Educational Psychology in Practice*, 17(1), 3–16.

Fulcher, G. (1990) *Disabling Policies? A Comparative Approach to Education Policy and Disability*. London: Falmer Press.

Garner, P. (1996) 'A la recherche du temps PRU', *Children and Society*, 10(3), 187–96.

Garner, P. (2000) 'Pretzel only policy? Inclusion and the real world of teacher education', *British Journal of Special Education*, 27(3), 111–16.

Garner, P. and Lewis, G. (1999) 'Standardising teachers: Attitudes towards national standards for those working with children with learning difficulties', *Early Child Development and Care*, 157, 97–107.

Garner, P. and Sandow, S. (eds) (1996) *Advocacy, Self-Advocacy and Special Needs*. London: David Fulton.

Giroux, H. (2000) *Stealing Innocence: Corporate Culture's War on Children*. New York: Palgrave.: New York

Glenny, G. (2005) 'Riding the dragon: Developing inter-agency systems for supporting inclusion', *Support for Learning*, 20(4), 167–75.

Goleman, D. (1996) *Emotional Intelligence. Why It Can Matter More Than IQ*. London: Bantam Books.

Hagood, M. (2001) *The Use of Art in Counselling Child and Adult Survivors of Sexual Abuse*. London: Jessica Kingsley.

Hallam, S. and Price, J. (1998) 'Can the use of background music improve the behaviour and academic performance of children with emotional and behavioural difficulties?', *British Journal of Special Education*, 25(2), 87–90.

Halstead, M. (ed.) (1994) *Parental Choice and Education: Principles, Policy and Practice*. London: Kogan Page.

Hendrick, H. (2005) *Child Welfare and Social Policy*. Bristol: The Policy Press.

Hewett, D. and Nind, M. (1998) (eds) *Interaction in Action: Reflections on the Use of Intensive Interaction*. London: David Fulton.

HM Government (1989) *The Children Act (1989)*. London: The Stationery Office.

Honey, H., Boughtwood, D., Clarke, S., Halse, C., Kohn, M. and Madden, S. (2008) 'Support for parents of children with anorexia: What parents want', *Eating Disorders*, 16(1), 40–51.

Howes, A. (2003) 'Teaching reforms and the impact of paid adult support on participation and learning in mainstream schools', *Support for Learning*, 18 (4), 147–53.

Johnson, M. (2002) 'Multi-sensory teaching of reading in mainstream settings', in J. Wearmouth, J. Soler, and G. Reid, *Addressing Difficulties in Literacy Development: Responses at Family, School, Pupil and Teacher Levels*. London: Routledge, 269–81.

Johnson, M. and Parkinson, J. (2002) *Epilepsy: A Practical Guide*. London: David Fulton.

Kaplan A., Gheen M. and Midgley, C. (2002) 'Classroom goal structure and student disruptive behaviour', *British Journal of Educational Psychology*, 72(2), 191–211.

Kenway, J. and Bullen, E. (2001). *Consuming Children: Education–Entertainment–Advertising*. Buckingham: Open University Press.

Kenworthy, J. and Whittaker, J. (2000) 'Anything to declare? The struggle for inclusive education and children's rights', *Disability and Society*, 15(2), 219–31.

Kirby, A. (2006) *Mapping SEN Routes through Identification to Intervention*. London: David Fulton.

Lambert, M. (2005) 'Conductive education: Links with mainstream schools', *Support for Learning*, 19(1), 31–7.

Layton, L. (2005) 'Special educational needs coordinators and leadership: A role too far?', *Support for Learning*, 20(2), 53–60.

Lewis, A. (1996) 'Summative National Curriculum assessment of primary aged children with special needs', *British Journal of Special Education*, 23(1), 9–14.

Lewis, I. and Vulliamy, G. (1980) 'Warnock or Warlock? The sorcery of definitions: The limitations of the Report on Special Education', *Educational Review*, 32(1), 3–10.

Lindsay, G. and Dockrell, J. (2002) 'Meeting the needs of children with speech, language and communication needs: A critical perspective on inclusion and collaboration', *Child Language Teaching and Therapy*, 18, 91–101.

Lundy, L. (2007) '"Voice" is not enough: Conceptualising Article 12 of the United Nations Convention on the Rights of the Child', *British Educational Research Journal*, 33(6), 927–42.

Lunt, I. and Norwich, B. (1999) *Can Effective Schools Be Inclusive Schools? Perspectives on Education Policy*. London: Institute of Education, University of London.

Machin, S., McNally, S. and Meghir, C. (2003) *Excellence in Cities: Evaluation of an Education Policy in Disadvantaged Areas*. Windsor: NFER.

Malik, A. (2008) 'A day in the life of a primary mentor', *Extended Schools Update*, February, London: DCSF.

McNamara, S. and Moreton, G. (1997) *Understanding Differentiation*. London: David Fulton.

Martin, A. (2006) 'Assessment using the P scales: Best fit – fit for purpose?', *British Journal of Special Education*, 33(2), 68–75.

Moberly, D., Waddle, J. and Duff, R. (2005) 'The use of rewards and punishment in early childhood classrooms', *Journal of Early Childhood Teacher Education*, 25(4), 359–66.

Morris, J. (1993) *Independent Lives: Community Care and Disabled People*. Basingstoke: Macmillan.

Morris, J., Abbott, D. and Ward, L. (2003) 'Disabled children and residential schools: The implications for local authority professionals', *British Journal of Special Education*, 20(2), 70–75.

National Curriculum Council (1989) *Curriculum Guidance 2: A Curriculum for All*. York: NCC.

National Curriculum Council (1992) *Curriculum Guidance 9: The National Curriculum and Children with Severe Learning Difficulties*. York: NCC.

Norwich, B. (2006) 'Dilemmas in inclusive education', in R. Cigman (ed.) *Included or Excluded? The Challenge of the Mainstream for some Children with SEN*. London: Routledge.

Norwich, B. and Kent, T. (2002) 'Assessing the personal and social development of pupils with special educational needs: Wider lessons for all', *Assessment in Education: Principles, Policy and Practice*, 9(1), 59–80.

Omdal, H. (2008) 'Including children with selective mutism in mainstream schools and kindergartens: Problems and possibilities', *International Journal of Inclusive Education*, 12(3), 301–15.

Parkes, J., Hill, N., Dolk, H. and Donelly, M. (2004) 'What influences physiotherapy use by children with cerebral palsy?', *Child: Care, Health and Development*, 30(2), 151–60.

Parsons, D., Hayden, C., Godfrey, R., Howlett, K. and Martin, T. (2002) *Outcomes in Secondary Education for Children Excluded from Primary School*, Research Report 271. London: DfES.

Peer, L. and Reid, G. (2003) *Introduction to Dyslexia*. London: David Fulton.

Potts, P. (1995) 'What's the use of history? Understanding educational provision for disabled students and those who experience difficulties in learning', *British Journal of Educational Studies*, 43(4), 398–411.

Poursanidou, K., Garner, P., Stephenson, R. and Watson, A. (2003) 'Educational difficulties and support needs of children following renal transplantation: Student, parent and teacher perspectives', *International Journal of Adolescence and Youth*, 11, 157–80.

Powell, S. and Tod, J. (2004) *A Systematic Review of how Theories Explain Learning Behaviour in School Contexts*. London: EPPI-Centre, SSRU.

Rayner, S. (2007) 'A teaching elixir, learning chimera or just fool's gold? Do learning styles matter?', *Support for Learning*, 22(1), 24–30.

Ripley, K. (2006) *First Steps to Emotional Literacy*. London: David Fulton.

Rodger, S. and Ziviani, J. (1999) 'Play-based occupational therapy', *Disability, Development and Education*, 46(3), 337–65.

Rogers, R., Tod, J., Powell, S., Parsons, C., Godfrey, R., Graham-Matheson, L., Carlson, A. and Cornwall, J. (2006) *Evaluation of the Special Educational Needs Parent Partnership Service in England*. London: DCSF.

Rosenblum S., Weiss P. and Parush S. (2003) 'Product and process evaluation of handwriting difficulties', *Educational Psychology Review*, 15(1), 41–81.

Russell, F. (2003) 'The expectations of parents of disabled children', *British Journal of Special Education*, 30(3), 144–9.

Sandow, S. (1994) *Whose Special Need?* London: Paul Chapman.

Schwartz, R. (2005). 'Literacy learning of at-risk first grade students in the Reading Recovery early intervention', *Journal of Educational Psychology*, 97, 257–67.

Shakespeare, T. (1998) 'Choices and rights: Eugenics, genetics and disability equality', *Disability and Society*, 13(5), 665–81.

Shanker, A. (1994) 'Inclusion and ideology', *Exceptional Parent*, 24(10), 39–40.

Siraj-Blatchford, I., Clarke, K. and Needham, M. (eds) (2007) *The Team Around the Child: Multi-Agency Working in the Early Years*. Stoke-on-Trent: Trentham Books.

Slee, R. (1996) 'Disability, social class and poverty: School structures and policing identities', in C. Christensen and F. Rizvi (eds) *Disability and the Dilemmas of Education and Justice*. Buckingham: Open University Press, 96–118.

Slee, R. (2000) 'Talking back to power. The politics of educational exclusion'. International Special Education Congress. Manchester, 24–28 July.

Sloper, P. (2004) 'Facilitators and barriers for coordinated multi-agency services', *Child Care, Health and Development*, 30(6), 571–80.

Soar, K., Gersch, I. and Lawrence, A. (2006) 'Pupil involvement in special educational needs disagreement resolution: A parental perspective', *Support for Learning*, 21(3), 149–55.

Solity, J. and Raybould, E. (1988) *The 1981 Education Act: A Positive Response*. Buckingham: Open University Press.

Sowell, T. (1995) *The Vision of the Anointed*. New York: Basic Books

Sprague, J., Walker, H., Stieber, S., Simonsen, B., Nishioka, V. and Wagner, L. (2001) 'Exploring the relationship between school discipline referrals and delinquency', *Psychology in the Schools*, 38(2), 197–206.

Sturmey, P. and Crisp, A. (1986) 'Portage guide to early education: A review of research', *Educational Psychology*, 6(2), 139–57.

Sutherland, G. (1981) 'The origins of special education', in W. Swann (ed.) *The Practice of Special Education*. Oxford: Blackwell/Open University Press, 93–103.

Tarr, J. and Thomas, G. (1997) 'The quality of special educational needs policies: Time for review?', *Support for Learning*, 12(1), 10–14.

Teacher Training Agency (1999) *National Special Educational Needs Specialist Standards*. London: TTA.

Tennant, G. (2007) 'IEPs in mainstream secondary schools: An agenda for research', *Support for Learning*, 22(4), 204–8.

Thomas, G., Walker, D. and Webb, J. (1998) *The Making of the Inclusive School*. London: Routledge.

Todd, L. (2006) *Partnerships for Inclusive Education: A Critical Approach to Collaborative Working*. London: Routledge.

Topping, K.J. (2001) *Peer Assisted Learning: A Practical Guide for Teachers.* Cambridge, MA: Brookline Books.

United Nations (1989) *The UN Convention on the Rights of the Child.* New York: UN.

United Nations Educational, Scientific and Cultural Organization (UNESCO) (1994) *The Salamanca Statement and Framework for Action on Special Needs Education,* Paris: UNESCO.

Vincent, C. and Ball, S. (2005) 'The "childcare champion"?: New Labour, social justice and the childcare market', *British Educational Research Journal,* 31(5), 557–70.

Wall, K. (2006) *Special Needs and the Early Years. A Practitioner's Guide.* London: Paul Chapman Educational Publishing.

Waterhouse, S. (2004) 'Deviant and non-deviant identities in the classroom: Patrolling the boundaries of the normal social world', *European Journal of Special Needs Education,* 19(1), 1–15.

Watkinson, A. (2008) *The Essential Guide for Competent Teaching Assistants.* London: David Fulton.

Wearmouth J. (2001) *Special Educational Provision: Meeting the Challenge in Schools.* London: Hodder and Stoughton.

Wearmouth, J. (2001) 'The Warnock report: The historical background', in J. Wearmouth (ed.) *Special Educational Provision in the Context of Inclusion.* London: David Fulton, 5–35.

Westwood, P. (2006) *Commonsense Methods for Children with Special Educational Needs.* London: Routledge Falmer.

Wheldall, K. (ed.) (1992) *Discipline in Schools: Psychological Perspectives on the Elton Report.* London: Routledge.

Wolfendale, S. (1999) 'Parents as partners in research and evaluation: Methodological and ethical issues and solutions', *British Journal of Special Education,* 26(3), 164–9.

Woolfson, L. and Grant, E. (2005) 'A comparison of special, regular and support teachers' beliefs about children's learning difficulties'. International Special Education Conference, 1–4 August, Strathclyde University.

Young Minds (2006) *Looking after the Mental Health of Looked After Children.* London: Young Minds.

USEFUL SEN-RELATED WEBSITES

These websites were accessed 13 December 2008.

Advisory Centre for Education: www.ace-ed.org.uk
Anti-bullying www.dfes.gov.uk/bullying
Asperger's Syndrome: www.aspergersyndrome.org/
Attention deficit (hyperactivity) disorder: www.addiss.co.uk/
Autism: www.nas.org.uk/
British Institute of Learning Disabilities: www.bild.org.uk/
British Psychological Society: www.bps.org.uk/index.cfm
Code of Practice 2001: http://publications.teachernet.gov.uk/
     eOrderingDownload/DfES per cent200581 per cent20200MIG2228.pdf
Disability/Disabled children: www.ncb.org.uk/Page.asp
Dyscalculia: www.bdadyslexia.org.uk/dyscalculia.html
Dyslexia: www.bdadyslexia.org.uk/
Dyspraxia: www.dyspraxiafoundation.org.uk/
Emotional and behavioural difficulties: www.behaviour4learning.ac.uk
Epilepsy: www.epilepsy.org.uk/
Every Child Matters: www.everychildmatters.gov.uk/
Hearing impairment: www.batod.org.uk/
Inclusive education: http://inclusion.ngfl.gov.uk/
Inclusive education: http://inclusion.uwe.ac.uk/csie/csiehome.htm
Literacy: www.literacytrust.org.uk
Mental handicap: www.mencap.org.uk/
Parent partnership: www.parentpartnership.org.uk/
Selective mutism www.selectivemutism.org/
Social and emotional aspects of learning: www.standards.dfes.gov.uk/pri-
     mary/publications/banda/seal/
Social disadvantage: www.barnardos.org.uk/
Social, emotional and behavioural difficulties: www.sebda.org/
Special educational needs: www.nasen.org.uk
Speech and language difficulties: www.ican.org.uk/
SEN Tribunal: www.sendist.gov.uk
Speech and language difficulties: www.afasic.org.uk/
Teachernet (SEN) www.teachernet.gov.uk/wholeschool/sen/
Training and Development Agency for Schools: www.tda.gov.uk/
Visual impairment: www.nbcs.org.uk/
Young Minds: www.youngminds.org.uk/

INDEX